WEST SUSSEX

Len Markham

COUNTRYSIDE BOOKS

NEWBURY BERKSHIRE

First published 2009
© Len Markham 2009

COUNTRYSIDE BOOKS
3 Catherine Road
Newbury, Berkshire

To view our complete range of books,
please visit us at
www.countrysidebooks.co.uk

ISBN 978 1 84674 122 7

*For Joyanne and Naomi
who have shown me many beautiful paths*

Maps by CJWT Solutions
Photographs by the author

Designed by Peter Davies, Nautilus Design
Produced through MRM Associates Ltd., Reading
Printed in Thailand

CONTENTS

Introduction

This book is written with fitness it mind, its carefully selected and graded routes all being designed as a useful contribution to healthy lifestyle changes such as quitting smoking and losing weight. A walking regime can, under the direction of a qualified doctor, also help in regaining strength and mobility after injury or illness.

Walking has numerous physical and psychological benefits. It is the least contrived and most natural exercise under the sun. It is free, it can be enjoyed in both winter and summer and, apart from sensible clothing and footwear, it requires no specialised equipment. It exercises the heart and lungs and improves stamina. It lowers blood pressure and keeps joints supple and it improves the complexion and releases endorphins, dissipating anxiety and tension. In addition, as a best-of-both-worlds bonus, regular walking helps boost the appetite, adding an extra zest to mealtimes whilst at the same time assisting in weight reduction.

Combined with a weight loss regime, walking can help in shedding the pounds. As a rough guide, walkers of around 11 stone in weight can expect to use up 100 calories plus per mile at a gentle amble, a brisker pace improving calorie expenditure by up to 50%. In calculating the calorie consumption for these walks, I have worked on the assumption that readers will not be content to dawdle and I have added extra values for walking up hills and crossing stiles. However, my figures have not been scientifically calculated and should be regarded only as a helpful guide.

It has been clinically proven in recent years that a brisk walk in the countryside has more beneficial effects in improving general well-being than any artificial stimulant or drug. Walking also has a spiritual dimension, the gentle re-acquaintance with the natural world infusing inner peace and serenity, offering a detox for the soul.

There is also one final benefit that I must share with you. Walking is the most companionable activity in the world. If, away from every modern distraction, you want to get to know someone and rekindle the wonderful art of friendly conversation, like Aristotle, stroll with them for a while. And if your fickle companions pull up their duvets and sleep on, follow my example and get yourself a friend who will be eager for the hills whatever the weather. As I have found out by daily pre-dawn scrapings at my bedroom door, a dog can be the most eager of walkers, your canine chum's unbridled appetite for daily exercise demanding you bounce out of bed and brave the elements come rain or shine.

As far as practicalities are concerned I would recommend cotton clothing, a warm woollen jumper for the colder days, a waterproof jacket and hat (useful for deflecting rays and rain!) and supple leather walking boots that provide ample ankle support and a good tread. Boots are particularly important on inclines as lots of the footpaths in West Sussex are on chalk and can, after wet weather, have the slippery consistency of cream cheese although chalk is highly porous and any surface water soon drains away. You will also have to negotiate muddy tracks, especially in dense woodlands frequented by horse riders, so good quality boots really are indispensable.

You should carry a haversack on all but the shortest walks, packing light, nutritious snacks and drinks (there are many inviting old pubs along the way but please do not linger too long and do watch the calories!) and, to heighten the pleasure and interest of days in the countryside, I would suggest investing in the appropriate quoted OS maps, binoculars, a camera and a field guide to birds and flowers. A pair of modern lightweight walking poles could also be useful. You may also wish, like me, to use a pedometer to calculate miles travelled and calorie burn.

Each of these walks is graded in an incremental fitness range of 1 to 3 according to length (they vary from ¾ mile to 8½ miles) and gradient difficulty, 1 classifying the least taxing routes and 3 the most strenuous. To aid walk selection, the routes are grouped and I give what I hope is a helpful grading analysis as follows:

Grade 1 – STROLL

Grade 2 – STRIDE

Grade 3 – HIKE

If you have only recently committed to a fitness programme, I would naturally recommend that you begin by tackling the grade 1 walks first, graduating to more demanding routes as your fitness and stamina improves. Slowly and gradually does it.

In devising this book, my first objective has been to design a regime that can offer a substantial contribution to personal fitness but I have also been mindful to maximise on the pleasurability of the experience. I would not want you hanging up your boots after the first outing! West Sussex is a beautiful county flush with magnificent coastal scenery, quiet heaths and woodlands, several gem estates in the care of the National Trust, and panoramic downland ablaze with spring and summer flowers. It also has an archaeological, historical, architectural, industrial and literary legacy that is second to none, these walks offering invigorating exercise in beautiful countryside but much else besides. The walks pass tumuli by the dozen and you can explore the sites of Bronze and Iron Age settlements and abandoned hill forts, one spectacular and challenging route visiting both the mysterious Cissbury and Chanctonbury rings in a single outing. Two of the walks have a Roman theme, stunning mosaics and other treasures in Fishbourne Palace and Bignor Villa setting the imperial scene for paths that in part follow the line of Stane Street – the old Roman road between Chichester and London. Some of the walks allow you to appreciate the largely forgotten industrial and commercial aspects of county history. You will discover ancient pits and oak glades where iron ore was dug and cannon were forged for use by the Royal Navy, two splendidly restored lengths of canal at Loxwood and Guildenhurst and a windmill at Shipley formerly belonging to the famous Sussex writer Hilaire Belloc, another of our walks visiting the author's former home in Slindon. And finally, at the beginning and end of the walks, there are inviting villages like the incomparable Fulking with its unique springheads, a host of other flint-walled hamlets with their thatched cottage roofs and old churches defining the vernacular architecture of West Sussex. My choice of twenty circuits encompasses all this with an enthusiasm I hope you will find catching.

As I said in my companion volumes, *Kiddiwalks in East Sussex*, *Kiddiwalks in West Sussex* and *Footpaths for Fitness in East Sussex*, in my own small way I have a mission to re-energise legs long atrophied by the sedentary age and to release on Sussex a tumult of heartily booted feet. Step out and conquer.

Finally, an admission. Although I have an impeccable walking pedigree underlined by the authorship of over a dozen walking guides on my native Yorkshire, I have at times, as a newcomer to Sussex, felt somewhat of an impostor. But that is in the past. Now, as a disciple of the Downs in all seasons, and as the author of four books on the county, I feel as though I have earned my spurs, my application to become a fully-fledged Saxon, as I believe natives of this part of the kingdom are called, being supported by a compatriot Yorkshireman – Arthur Beckett - who came to Sussex in the 1870s and made the place his own. His was a passionate voice for the preservation of the unique downland landscape. The first president of the South Downs Society and the influential editor of the *Sussex County Magazine*, Beckett wrote his own stirring tributes to his adopted home in *Spirit of the Downs, The Wonderful Weald, Sussex at War* and *Poems of Peace*. I hope this little book, interspersed as it is with a sprinkling of my own poems, keeps up his good work.

Len Markham

Publisher's Note

We hope that you obtain considerable enjoyment from this book; great care has been taken in its preparation. Although at the time of publication all routes followed public rights of way or permitted paths, diversion orders can be made and permissions withdrawn.

We cannot, of course, be held responsible for such diversion orders and any inaccuracies in the text which result from these or any other changes to the routes, nor any damage which might result from walkers trespassing on private property. We are anxious though that all details covering the walks are kept up to date and would therefore welcome information from readers which would be relevant to future editions.

The simple sketch maps that accompany the walks in this book are based on notes made by the author whilst checking out the routes on the ground. They are designed to show you how to reach the start, to point out the main features of the overall circuit and they contain a progression of numbers that relate to the paragraphs of the text.

However, for the benefit of a proper map, we do recommend that you purchase the relevant Ordnance Survey sheet covering your walk. The Ordnance Survey maps are widely available, especially through booksellers and local newsagents.

A Swim Before Breakfast

Apple-cheeked and panting at the topmost yard,
And there, close by – the sea!
Onward, beaming and breathless,
Bounding along like the Skegness salt.

Gobbling up the ground, hair a-blowing,
Quaffing and relishing the chill May air,
Running now on downward plunge,
A giddy prance through sea-pinks dancing.

Airborne, the briefest flight to beach,
A thud, a tumble, a gritty roll and up – sprinting,
A beach-sprung-rock-pool-crashing dash,
To surf and splash.

Unzipped, a button-bursting frenzy,
The pimpled flesh ventured to the foam,
Breath held and braced,
A spring, a dive and Neptune's creamy broth caressing.

Tingling and shaking like a dog,
Then dressed on dampened skin,
A race to sweetheart's door,
The whiff of ham and eggs tugging me all the way.

Len Markham

(Scribbled while still shivering with the tang of
Cuckmere Haven in my nostrils)

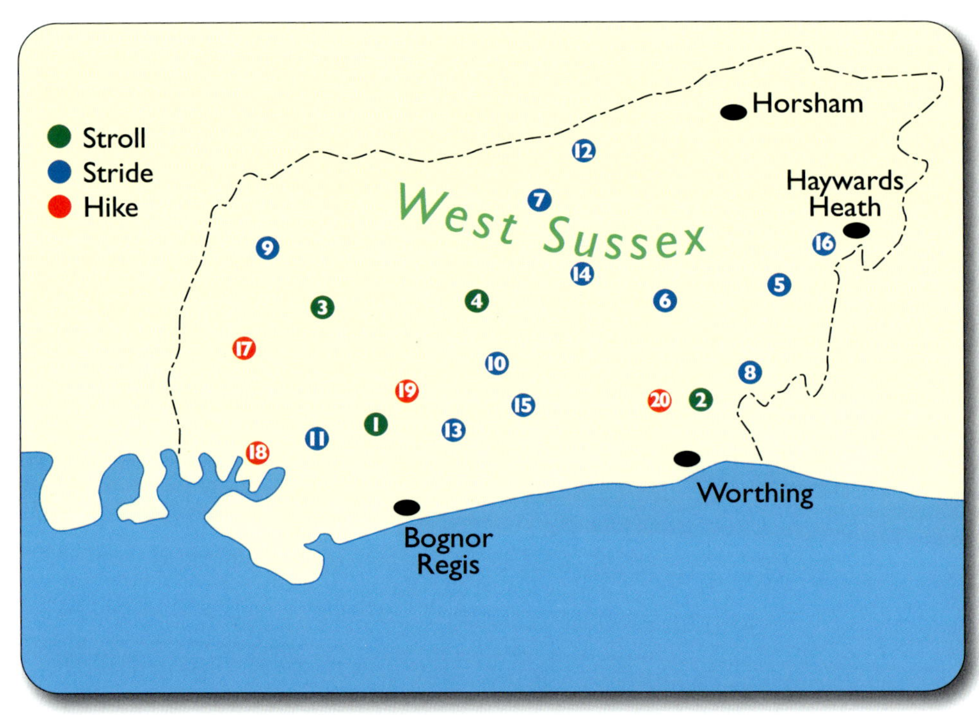

Area map showing location of the walks

1 St Roche's Hill

A Glorious Grandstand!

FOOTPATHS FOR FITNESS

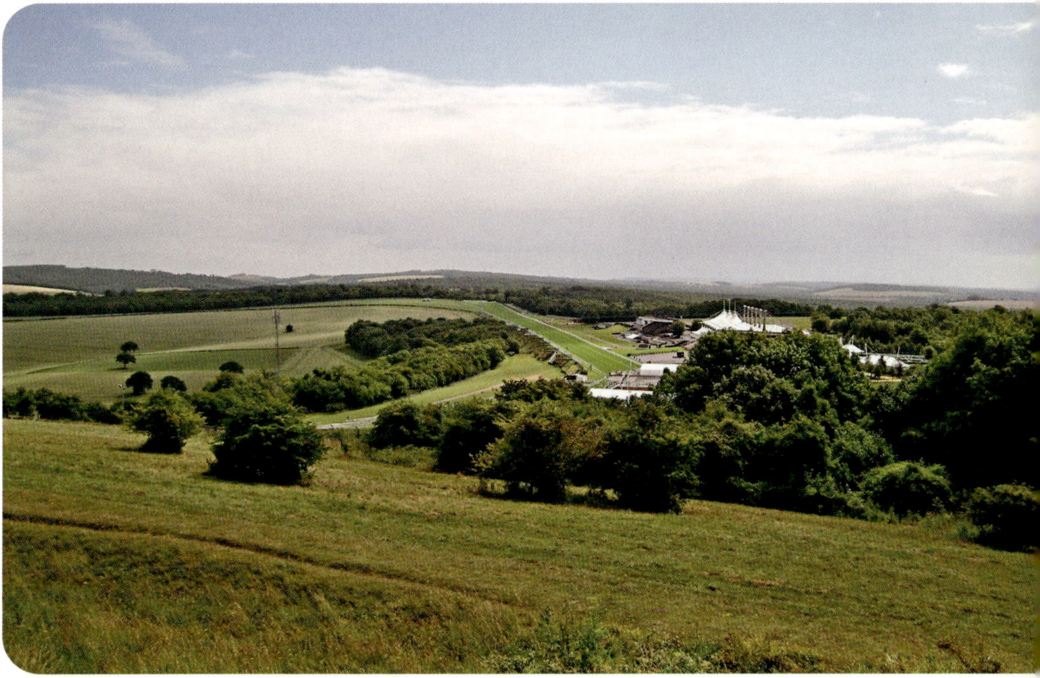

■ *The view over Goodwood racecourse* ■

Given a telescope and a winning treble, there is no finer place to count your winnings in the world, lofty St Roche's Hill offering a grandstand view of glorious Goodwood racecourse … for free! The hill is the site of a 6,000-year-old Neolithic camp, later used by Iron Age settlers as a hill fort. Later still it was the location of a 14th-century chapel and in the 18th century a windmill was built here, a fire claiming the structure in 1773. Nearby is the Monarch's Way, so-called in memory of King Charles II who used the route to escape from arrest after his defeat at the Battle of Worcester in 1651. Commanding magnificent eagle-eye views of the countryside and the sea, this walk is an ideal introduction to our fitness regime, Sussex's own floral emblem, the round-headed rampion – the rare crowning glory known as the Pride of Sussex – waving from the ramparts like some mini standard.

> **GRADE: 1**
> **ESTIMATED CALORIE BURN: 110**

Description: The shortest route in the book; a walking aperitif, circumnavigating this historic and iconic hill.
Distance: ¾ mile.
Time: 30 minutes.
Gradient: 15% of the route. One short, steep climb at point 1. No stiles.
Underfoot: The well-worn footpaths are mostly flat and even all the way.
Starting point: The free parking area below the hill. GR 879114.
How to get there: St Roche's Hill is around 4 miles north of Chichester. From the A286, turn off eastwards in Mid Lavant, going through East Lavant on a minor road. Turn left on Kennel Hill and pass the entrance to Goodwood racecourse, going left round the bend to the parking area.
OS map: Explorer 120 Chichester, South Harting & Selsey.
Refreshments: There are no formal refreshment facilities to hand but bring champagne and a picnic basket and watch the winners go by!

1 Leave the car park, going left, and cross the road right on the bend, walking up the steps and steering right, following the public footpath sign to a kissing gate. Go through left uphill, climbing to the left of the communications tower.

2 Go left on the earthwork embankment and follow this round right in a circle, passing the second communications tower, back to the end of point 1.

3 Go left back to the start.

■ *Looking north from St Roche's Hill* ■

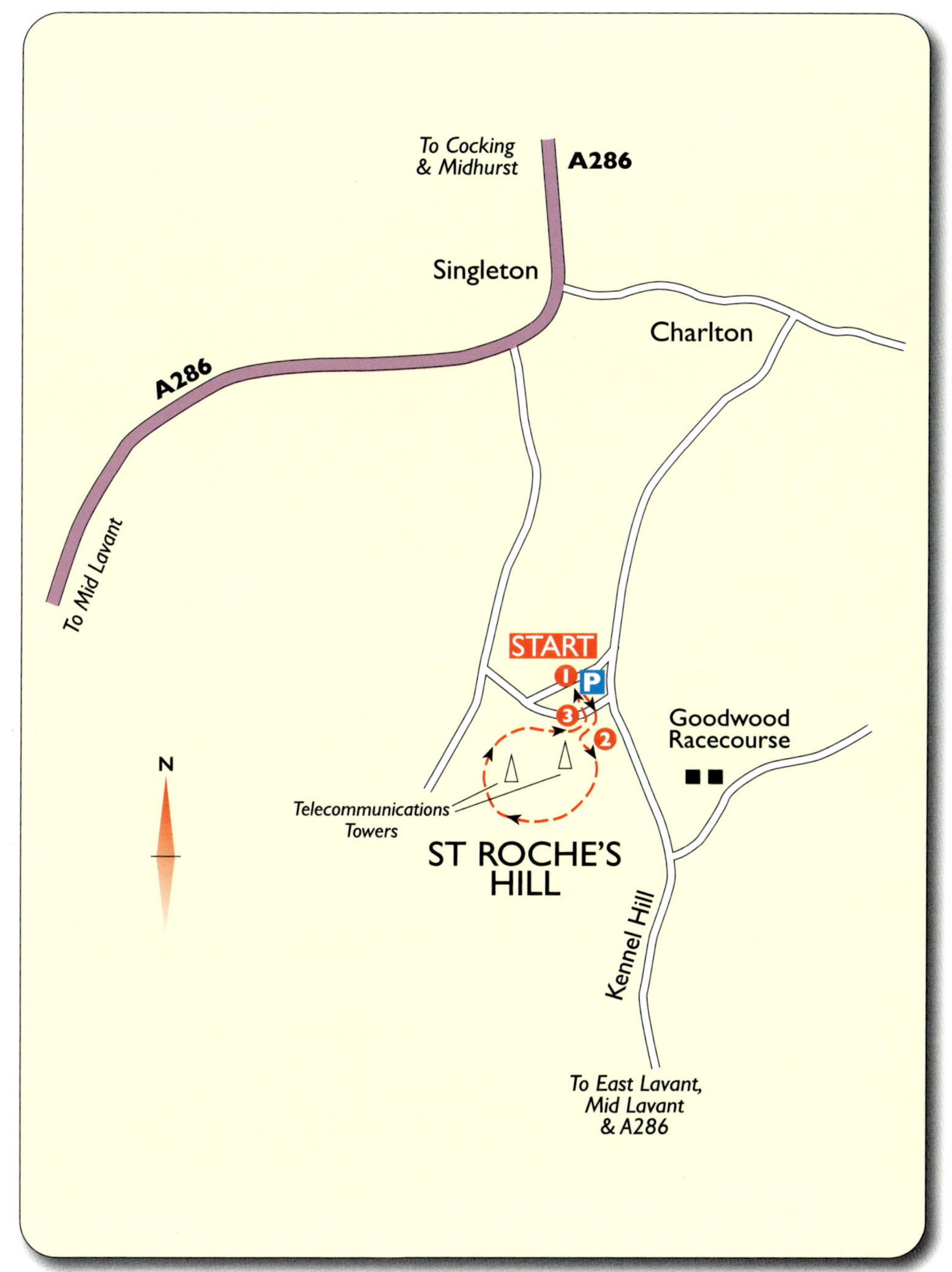

To Cocking & Midhurst
A286
Singleton
Charlton
A286
To Mid Lavant
START
P
Goodwood Racecourse
Telecommunications Towers
ST ROCHE'S HILL
Kennel Hill
To East Lavant, Mid Lavant & A286
N

■ *One of Bramber's fine houses* ■

At a strategic crossing of the River Adur, Bramber was embattled by the Normans in 1073, one of William's conquering knights raising a mighty fortress that presided over a once-thriving port and lucrative salt works. Today, only the crumbling castle keep and the outlines of the old salt pans remain although two of our route-visited churches and a fine selection of beautifully preserved period houses in the village honour an illustrious past that attracts hosts of visitors. This historical circuit passes a cluster of medieval dwellings, the site of the salt works alongside the **Adur**, and moves on to the repose of the wonderfully sequestered priory church of St Peter. Our route crosses the river on a footbridge, returning to the

GRADE: 1
ESTIMATED CALORIE BURN: 260

Description: A fascinating village, riverside, water meadows, church-yards and castle precincts ramble, in a delightful part of West Sussex.
Distance: 1¾ miles.
Time: 2 hours.
Gradient: 5% of the route – in the vicinity of the church of St Peter and later at Bramber Castle.
Underfoot: Easy and well-defined village and riverside footpaths.
Starting point: Park in the free car park off The Street in Bramber. GR 187107.
How to get there: Bramber is on the A283 around 4 miles north-west of Shoreham-by-Sea.
OS map: Explorer 122 Brighton & Hove
Refreshments: The Castle Hotel opposite the car park serves good bar meals.

village through National Trust grounds and on under the shadow of the gaunt remains of Bramber Castle to the church of St Nicholas. Contemporary with the castle, it miraculously survives.

1 Turn left from the car park along **The Street** – passing the half-timbered and jettied circa 1470 St Mary's House. After 100 yards, turn right, following a public footpath sign, crossing a bridge and going left towards the river. Go left through a kissing gate and left on the bank to the bridge and turn right over the bridge.

2 Cross the road opposite the pub and walk on upstream on the bank, going through a kissing gate into **Saltings Field**. This stretch of the river is home to kingfishers, herons and cormorants, the still-visible old saltern mounds providing a habitat for rare plants. Swing left and right to the pumping station and arc right and then left after 50 yards by a post up the bank to find a footpath. Turn left at the bottom of the gardens towards the church of St Peter. The building was formerly a Benedictine priory although the structure was almost completely rebuilt in 1308.

3 Go left down the steps back towards the river, following the signpost, and cross a footbridge, heading right towards the bigger footbridge over the river. Cross left and follow the footpath sign forward across a meadow.

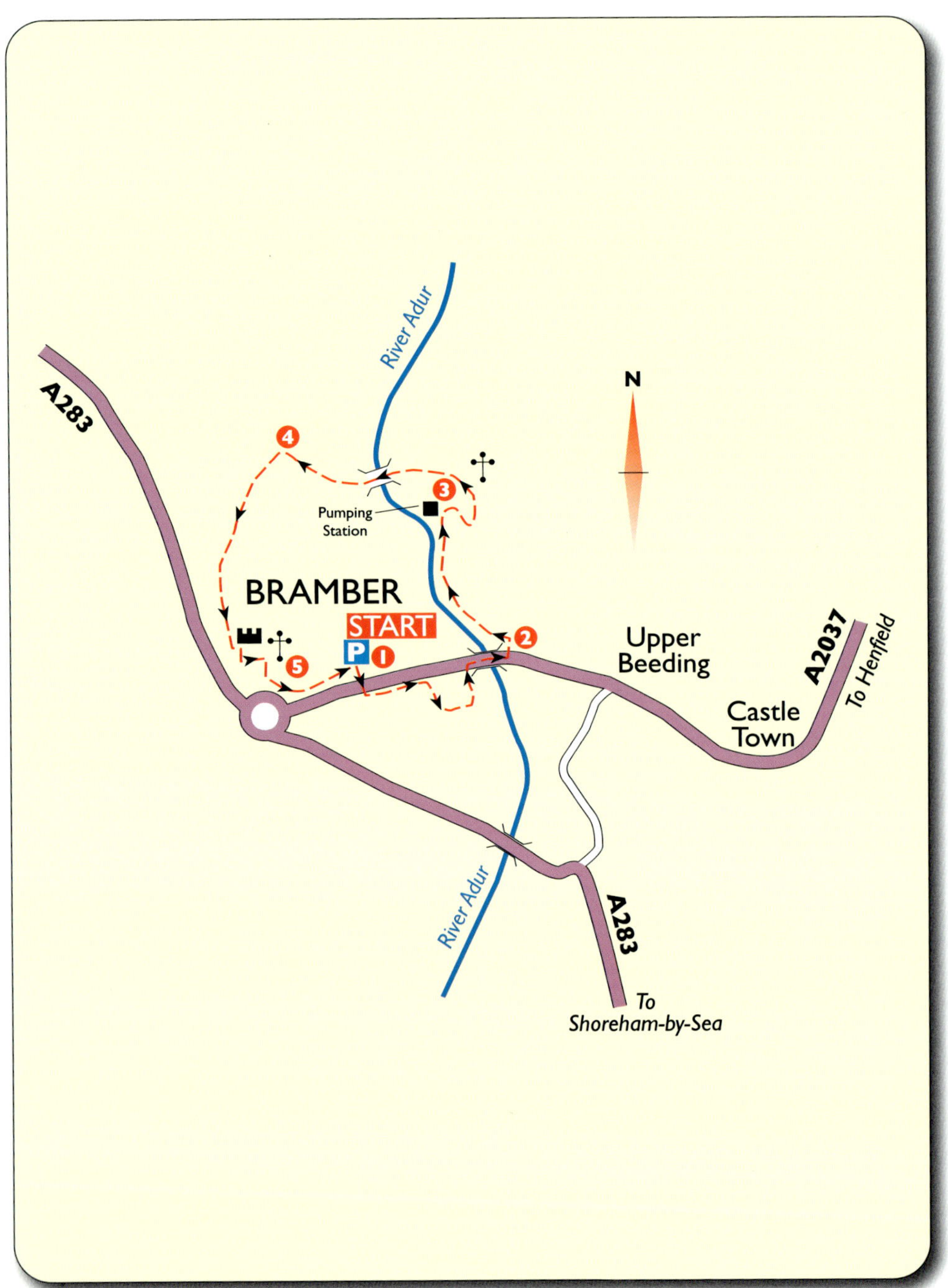

River Adur
A283
N
4
3
Pumping Station
BRAMBER
START
P 1
5
2
Upper Beeding
A2037
To Henfield
Castle Town
River Adur
A283
To Shoreham-by-Sea

■ *Bramber's ruined castle keep* ■

4 Go left at the next signpost and walk on a path at the side of the estate towards the castle, entering the castle grounds left and keeping right of the old keep. Go left into the churchyard of St Nicholas through a gate and go right and then left through the lychgate dropping down to **The Street**.

5 Go left back to the car park.

3 Iping
Rother Ramble

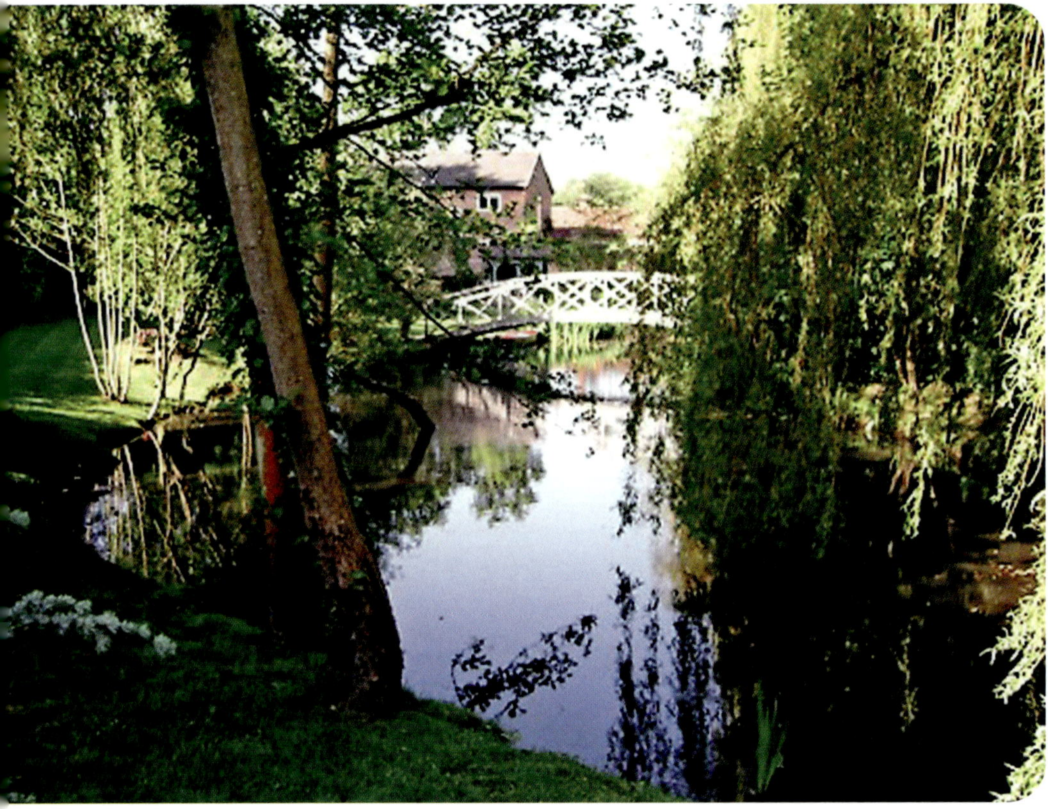

■ *The glorious River Rother* ■

Exploring an area famous for polo horses – the famous Cowdray Park is nearby on the outskirts of Midhurst – this leisurely walk, along the twin banks of the River Rother, shows you what the thoroughbreds do on their days off, their elegant munching adding a regal sparkle to a walk between two churches. Both dedicated to St Mary, the churches overlook ancient bridges, our route following a river that, like some sultry lady, hides behind a mantilla of leaves. Through equestrian pastures, we cross the line of an old Roman road and a footbridge over the Hammer Stream, the name alluding to the iron industry that once dominated here.

GRADE: 1
ESTIMATED CALORIE BURN: 325

Description: A short and easy riverside ramble between two historical settlements.
Distance: 1¾ miles.
Time: 1 hour.
Gradient: The route is generally flat. Four stiles.
Underfoot: The riverside paths are easily negotiated although some rights-of-way across meadows are indeterminate so keep straight ahead without deviation across fields, particularly in the middle part of Point 1.
Starting point: The parking area at the entrance to St Mary's church, just beyond the bridge. GR 854230.
How to get there: Iping is 2½ miles north-west of Midhurst, just north of the A272 on a single-track road.
OS map: Explorer 133 Haslemere & Petersfield.
Refreshments: There are no refreshment opportunities along or near the route but the Hamilton Arms in the adjacent village of Stedham is recommended for bar meals.

At the halfway point, Chithurst Manor and the 11th-century St Mary's – it is thought to have been built on a pagan burial mound – present a tranquil scene, our return path passing Iping's weir and its converted mill.

1 Go through the gate into the churchyard, following the public footpath sign, and walk along the path, weaving right and left to a stile, crossing into a meadow. Steer left into the field corner. Go through a gate, following a public footpath sign, and swing right. There is a first glimpse of the **Rother** here. Follow the yellow arrow marker on the post left and cross a footbridge over the **Hammer Stream**, heading up and across a meadow to the left of the stable. Cross a second stile, keeping straight forward, and swing right between the fences towards the farmstead. Swing right and left through the two gates, following the yellow arrow marker on the post, and continue to the lane.

2 Go left on the lane, passing **St Mary's** and cross the bridge over the **Rother**. Pass **Wembridge House** and **Lassington** and the Trotton village sign and walk on for 150 yards.

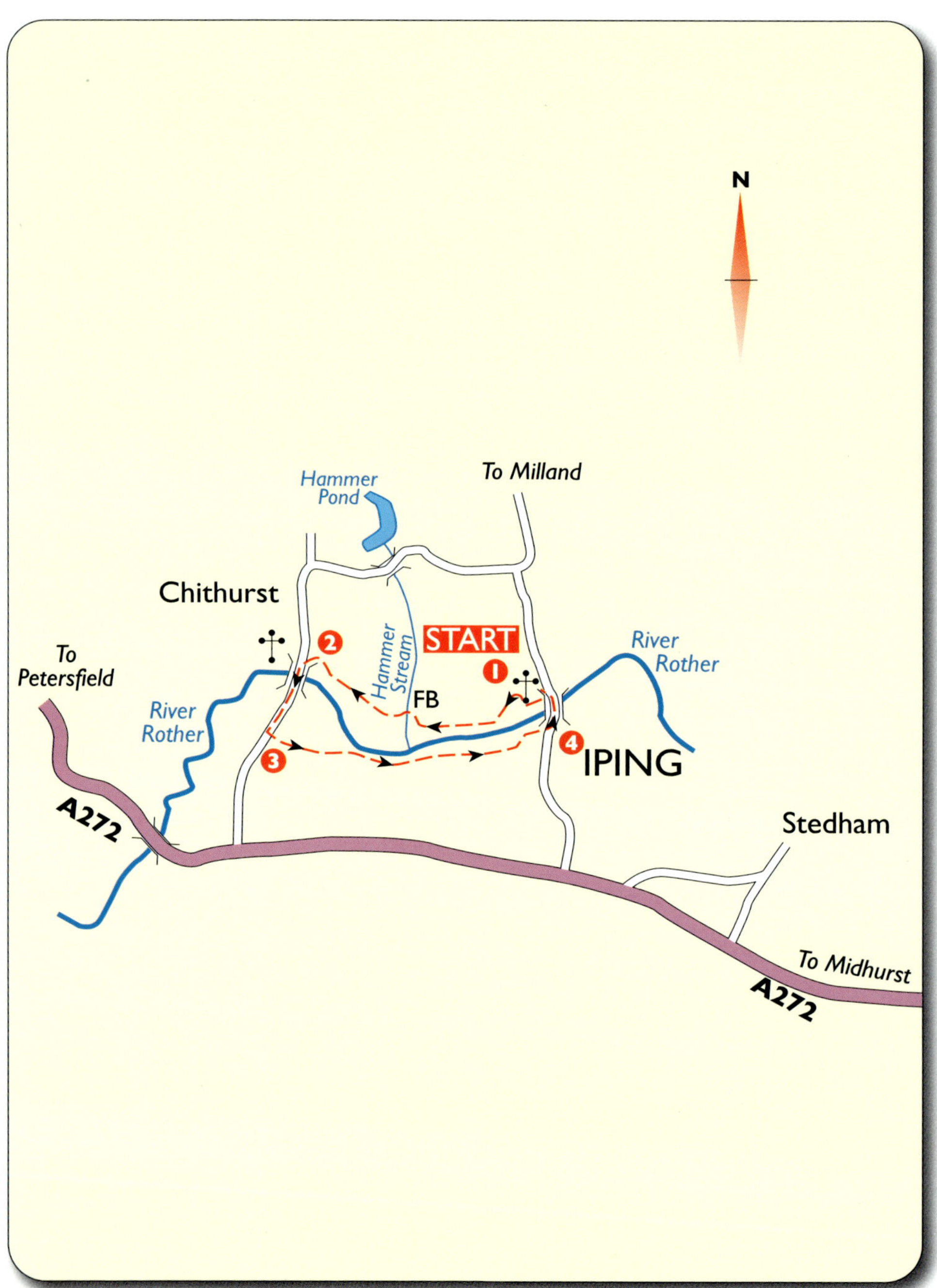

N
Hammer Pond
To Milland
Chithurst
START
Hammer Stream
River Rother
To Petersfield
River Rother
FB
2
3
4
IPING
Stedham
A272
To Midhurst
A272

■ *St Mary's church, Chithurst* ■

3 Go left off the lane, following the public footpath sign, crossing a footbridge. Walk on between fences and keep straight forward at the field edge. There are further views of the **Rother** deep in the valley below. Follow the next field down. In the field corner, cross a third stile, following the yellow arrow marker into the wood. Cross a footbridge and weave left, crossing a rickety fourth stile right. Follow the field edge down and in the field corner go left and right through a gate to the lane.

4 Turn left on the lane, crossing the bridge, and continue back to the start point.

4 Petworth
A Walk in the Park

■ *In the grounds of Petworth Park* ■

Walks in the environs of Petworth House** were conceived by its original owners as the most decorous of strolls on carefully laid out paths – once jealously guarded and strictly private – between herbaceous borders, classical temples and ponds, leading on to tracks through a substantial deer park for more adventurous guests. Now under the impeccable guardianship of the National Trust, the boundaries of the stately home's extensive grounds have been cleared of their man traps to offer modern visitors the most relaxed of perambulatory delights for free.

GRADE: 1
ESTIMATED CALORIE BURN: 470

Description: Markham's environmentally friendly equivalent of the red carpet – a stately orbit of Petworth House grounds on velvety green paths and formal tracks.
Distance: 3 miles.
Time: 1½ hours.
Gradient: There is one short climb in Point 1. No stiles.
Underfoot: Given dry weather, you could do this walk in slippers.
Starting point: Park in the pay and display car park around 1½ miles north of the house, signposted off the A283. GR 968238.
How to get there: Petworth is on the A272/A283 north-west of Arundel, midway between Midhurst and Pulborough.
OS map: Explorer 133 Haslemere & Petersfield.
Refreshments: The margins of the Upper Pond are picnic perfect.

This circuit urges us on a grand tour of undulating grounds laid out by Capability Brown, taking in the delights of the big house and two substantial ponds. There are magnificent views all around, the regal landscape inspiring the canvas of one of Petworth's most famous house guests – the artist Turner – and you will encounter a surprising amount of wildlife, including grebes, coots, moorhens, dabchicks, Canada geese and exotic waterfowl.

1 Turn left from the car park and pass the information board, veering left on a track towards the distant pond. Keep left of the **Lower Pond** on a path and swing left away from the pond, heading for the fenced foxhound compound. Pass the kennels and steer right uphill on a turfy track joining a stony track and swinging left by a wall. You will notice hereabouts the massive trunks of fallen trees, laid low by destructive storms. A vigorous re-planting programme has been undertaken in recent years but some of Brown's specimen leviathans still grace the park. Continue right to the house, swinging right by the ha-ha.

2 Keep swinging right and turn right on a track heading away from the monumental iron gates. Continue towards the **Upper Pond**.

3 Turn right towards the pond and its boathouse in the distance and veer left, following the curving bank to the pond end. To the left is a feature grove of yew.

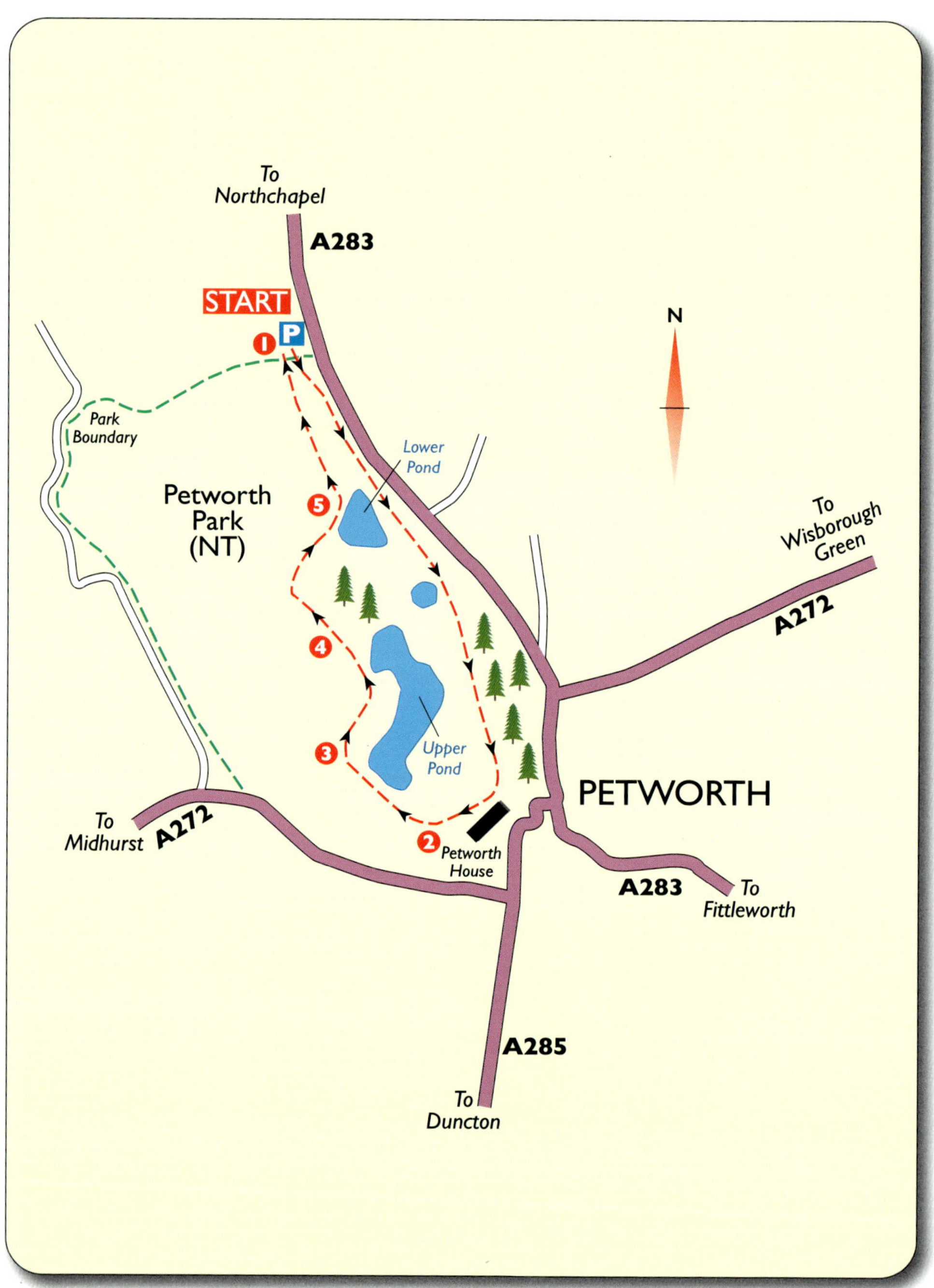

To Northchapel
A283
START
P
1
Park Boundary
Petworth Park (NT)
Lower Pond
N
To Wisborough Green
A272
5
4
3
Upper Pond
2
Petworth House
PETWORTH
To Midhurst
A272
A283
To Fittleworth
A285
To Duncton

■ *Upper Pond, with its memorial to a faithful companion* ■

4 Swing left into the deer pastures away from the black fence – this most secluded part of the park is where the deer like to graze – and swing right on a green path arcing round the wooded hillock towards the **Lower Pond**.

5 Go left on a path and swing right back to the parking area.

5 Cuckfield
Cuckoo Trails

Holy Trinity church passed on the route

Named after the cuckoos that once sang their hypnotic songs in the glades nearby, dapper Cuckfield reached the zenith of its importance in the days of the coach and four. On the busy route between London and Brighton, its coaching inns prospered but the iron horse was driven away to nearby Haywards Heath by outraged residents and, in comparison with its neighbour, the town slumbered. This moderately easy walk begins in the High Street, leading on through an extensive churchyard. There are distant views of the Downs for most of the way, our route using ancient tracks, woodland and grassy paths beset with bluebells and wood anemones in the early spring.

GRADE: 2
ESTIMATED CALORIE BURN: 515

Description: A gentle to moderate amble in pleasant countryside in view of the Downs, using lanes, tracks and woodland paths.
Distance: 3 miles.
Time: 1½ hours.
Gradient: 15% of the route, which is generally flat, although there are some gentle ascents near watercourses.
Underfoot: Some muddy patches may be encountered near stream margins and along the edges of low-lying meadows. Eight stiles.
Starting point: Park on High Street above the Queen's Hall. There is a car park on Broad Street (down the High Street and left) but this is operated under a disc system (discs available for purchase at local shops) valid for only two hours. GR 305248.
How to get there: Cuckfield is immediately west of Haywards Heath and is easily accessed off the A272.
OS map: Explorer 135 Ashdown Forest.
Refreshments: There is a wide choice of dining options in Cuckfield, including several cafés and pubs.

1 Walk down the **High Street** and at the bend, go left just before **King's Mews** along **Church Street**. Pass under the lych-gate and enter the extensive church grounds, keeping straight forward on a path through the churchyard with its interesting array of tombstones, one of their more lively companions – a magnificent sequoia – competing with the church spire in its quest for heaven. Exit via a metal kissing gate and turn right on a track.

2 Go next left on a track, following a public footpath sign. Swing left at the farm shop and continue, crossing a stile and the A272.

3 Following the public footpath sign, keep straight forward to the right of the treatment works and cross a second and a third stile, following the fence down to a rusted kissing gate (signpost grounded) at the corner of the treatment works. Go forward hedgeside and down and, keeping to the hedgeside, cross a fourth stile, dropping down to pass over a footbridge over a stream in a wood. Weave up left and right to the back of the cottage and go right on a track at the woodland edge. Ignore the first direction signs and walk on for 20 yards to the track bend, going left over a fifth stile, following a public footpath sign, keeping to the top end of the wood. Swing

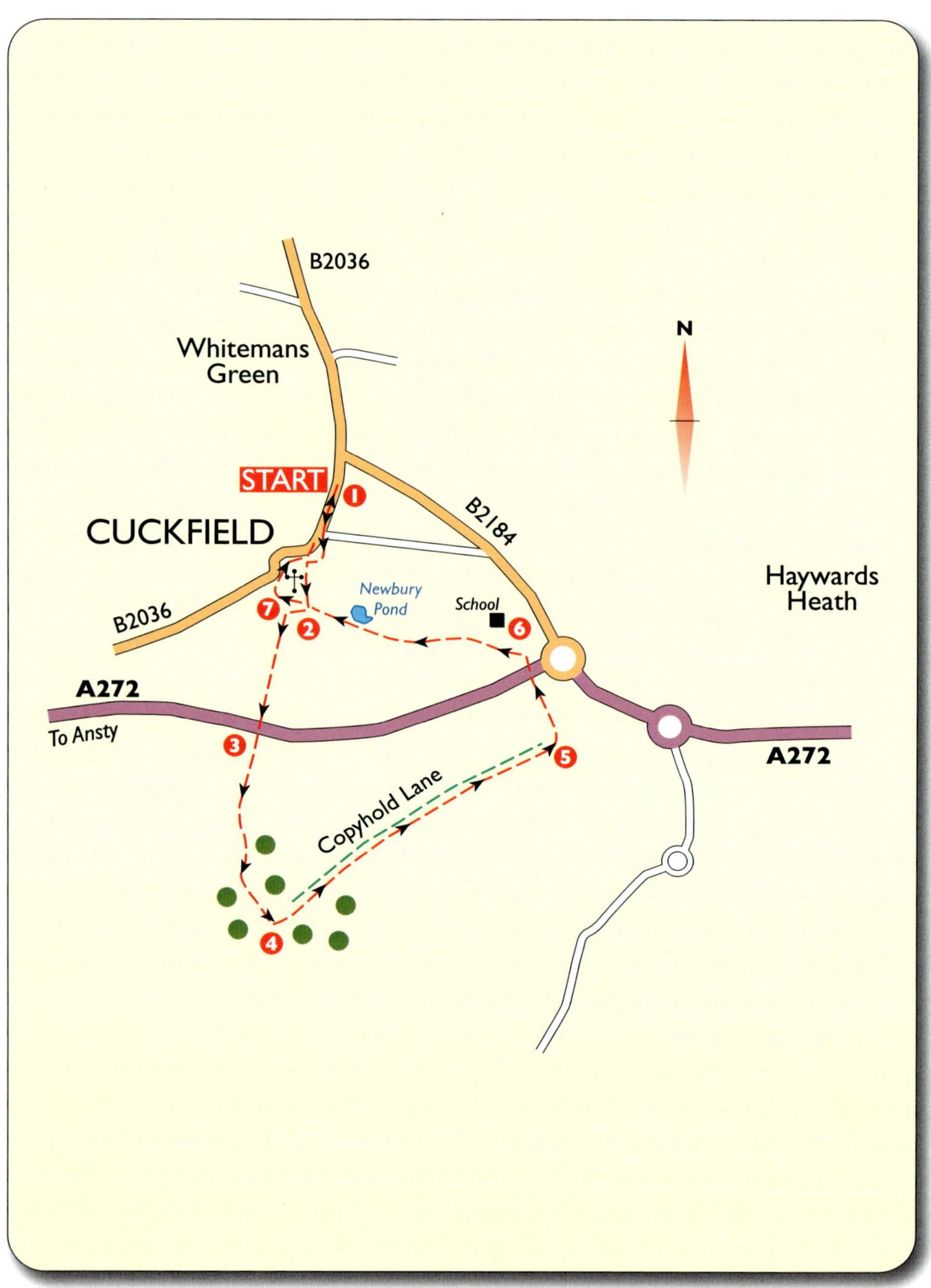
B2036
Whitemans
Green
START
CUCKFIELD
B2184
N
B2036
Newbury
Pond
School
Haywards
Heath
A272
To Ansty
A272
Copyhold Lane
1
7
2
3
6
5
4

Copyhold Lane is lined like a jewel box

left 50 yards before the field corner into the wood and cross a footbridge, continuing to the lane.

4 Go left, cross the bridge and fork immediately left again off the bend, following the public bridleway sign on a rising path. Leave the path opposite **Copyhold Cottage** and keep forward along the quiet **Copyhold Lane**. Pass **Lodge Farm** and a dozen or so large houses to the left and right, continuing to the direction signs.

5 Turn left, following the public footpath signs on a path between gardens, continuing to cross a sixth stile and the A272.

6 Keep straight forward, following the public footpath sign. At the tri-directional sign, turn left on a path, walking on at the perimeter of the school playing fields. Cross a seventh stile and keep to the meadow edge to cross an eighth stile in the field corner. Keep forward, following the public footpath sign, passing **Newbury Pond** and steering left uphill towards the churchyard.

7 Turn right through the kissing gate used on the outward route and go next left on a pathway and exit the churchyard. Turn right on the lane and go next right, re-entering the churchyard through a gate and passing left of the chapel. The fenced memorial to the left of the chapel honours Ernest Payne, a pioneer in X-ray research. Walk on to visit the church. **Holy Trinity** is over 900 years old. The uniquely glorious ceiling may be viewed in a mirror without straining your neck, its original panels dating from the 15th century. On the walls of the south chapel are thirteen monuments to members of the Burrell family who made a fortune as ironmasters (see Walk 16, West Hoathly). Leave the church and return to the parking area.

In the Footsteps of Hilaire Belloc

■ *The famous mill in Shipley* ■

As timeless as flint, the poetic and literary legacy of Hilaire Belloc is nowhere more enduring than in Shipley – the village he called home. He came to this halcyon spot on a bicycle in 1906, towing his new wife behind in a wickerwork trailer, the couple instantly falling in love with King's Land and its adjoining windmill. Belloc wrote prodigiously in his new and inspiring abode and he wandered long distances on foot, his book *The Four Men* taking us on a cross-country tour of the entire county. This more

GRADE: 2
ESTIMATED CALORIE BURN: 515

Description: Alive with birdsong (come in May like me and you might hear the cuckoo), an away-from-it-all ramble down quiet lanes and tracks and over farmland.
Distance: 3¼ miles.
Time: 1½ hours.
Gradient: There is a slight incline at the end of point 6 and a steady ascent on the lane in point 7. Four stiles.
Underfoot: The route is mainly on bridleways and in some places the passage of horses can make the paths muddy after prolonged rain.
Starting point: The parish council parking bays adjacent to Kings Land and the mill on Red Lane, Shipley. GR 144219.
How to get there: Shipley is off the A272, around 7 miles west of the A23 at Bolney.
OS map: Explorer 134 Crawley & Horsham.
Refreshments: The award-winning Countryman Inn is just off the route to the right at point 7 down Smithers Hill Lane. The inn is renowned for its use of fresh fish, free-range eggs and poultry and local game, and has a kitchen garden for use in the summer months.

leisurely walk around his own home-fields begins at the windmill, which has been restored as a tribute to Belloc, the mill – it will be familiar to millions of TV viewers as the fictional home of detective Jonathan Creek – also remembering another great writer who settled locally north of the village – Wilfred Scarwen Blunt.

Down tracks and lanes, flower-filled in season, the route offers glimpses of Belloc's beloved Sussex Downs and there are some greening remnants of the iron industry that also figure in his work. The farmland hereabouts is in the process of what could be termed wilderness nurturing; the enlightened Knepp Castle estate, which owns 3,000 local acres, restoring streams, ponds and hedgerows and gradually introducing wild, free-roaming fallow deer, Tamworth pigs, Exmoor ponies and longhorn cattle. Watch this wide-open space!

1 Go left past **King's Land**. Belloc lived in the property from 1906 until 1953 and wrote many of his novels, essays, poems and histories in the house. Continue for 200 yards to the bridleway sign and go left through the gate on the access lane, swinging left and right on a track, passing **Shipley Mill**.

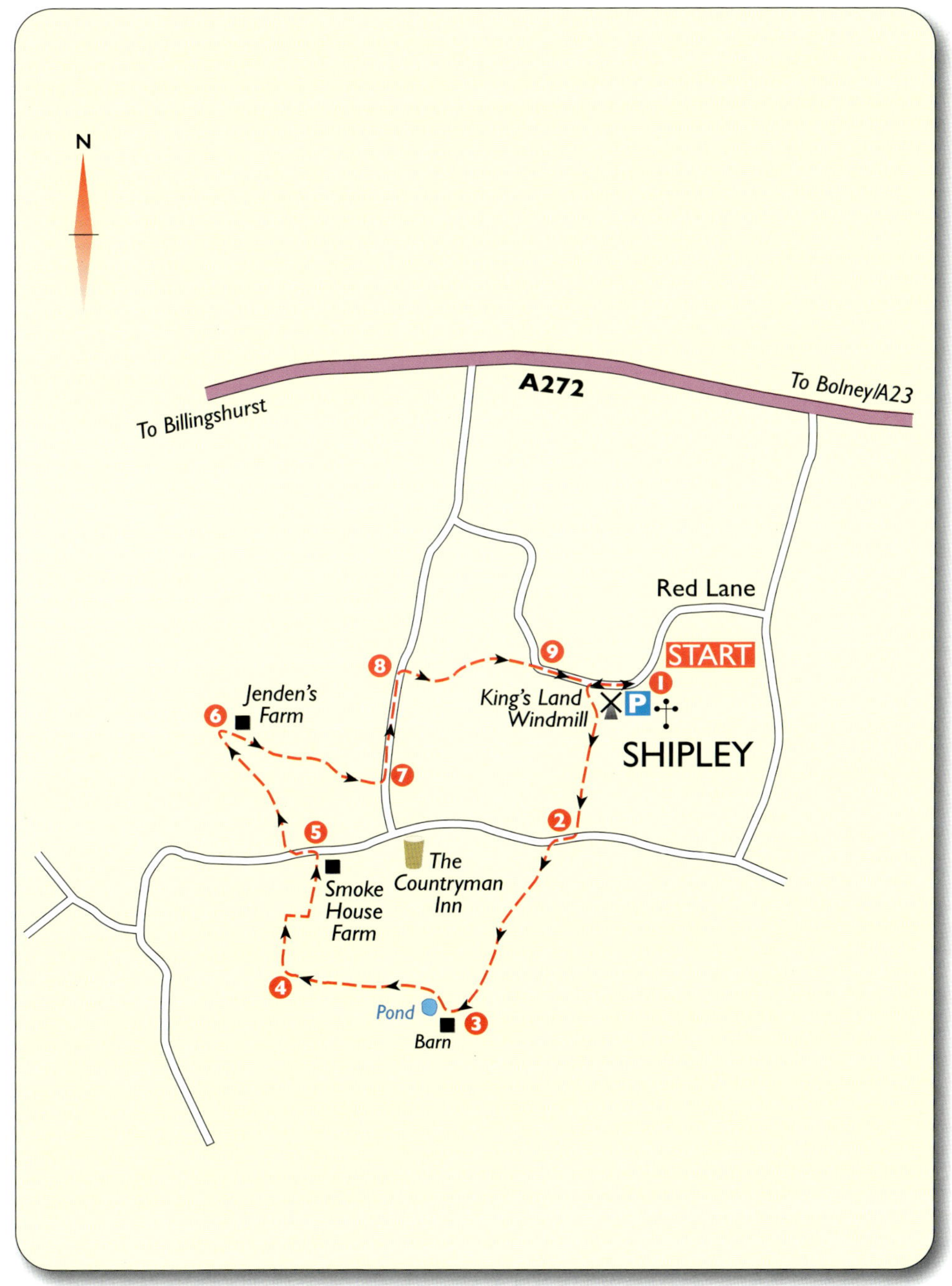
N
To Billingshurst
A272
To Bolney/A23
Red Lane
START
8
9
Jenden's
Farm
6
King's Land
Windmill
1
SHIPLEY
7
2
5
Smoke
House
Farm
The
Countryman
Inn
4
Pond
3
Barn

This is an eight-sided smock mill, so-called because of its resemblance to an agricultural worker's smock. It was built in 1879 and is open to the public on the first, second and third Sundays in the month, Easter to October, and Bank Holiday Mondays, 2 pm to 5 pm. Follow the public bridleway sign on a track, crossing the footbridges and walk on to the lane.

2 Turn right on the lane for 200 yards and go left on a track, following a public bridleway sign. Keep forward at the yellow **Toll Rides** sign, ignoring the track to the left, and swing right by the stream to the tri-directional sign by the lower barn and a pond.

3 Go right, following the public footpath sign. Swing right at the top of the bank, cross a stream on a bridge and go left, following a public footpath sign. There are views of the Downs from this location. Continue hedgeside for three fields and in the third field corner walk on for 20 yards.

4 Go right over a planked bridge, following a public footpath sign hedgeside. Go right in the field corner, following a public footpath sign for 200 yards to the next direction post. Go left over a concrete bridge, following a public footpath sign, walking on hedgeside towards **Smoke House Farm**. Go left and right of the shed over a stile and a planked bridge to the lane.

5 Go left on the lane for 180 yards and go right through a gate, following a public footpath sign, heading for the field corner. Go through a kissing gate and walk on hedgeside. Go through a gate, following a public footpath sign, crossing a field and keeping to the right of the big tree, heading for the corner and **Jenden's Farm**.

6 In the corner, stay in the field and turn sharp right, following the public footpath sign, walking on parallel with the farm access road and the black fence. Go right by the pool and cross stiles two and three, swinging right to a farm bridge. Swing left over the bridge and walk on right alongside the ditch, continuing to a footpath sign. Walk away from the ditch, veering right up a slight rise, crossing a fourth stile at the field edge over a planked bridge to **Smithers Hill Lane**.

7 Go left on **Smithers Hill Lane** on a gentle ascent, continuing to the **Jenden's Farm** access.

8 Walk on past the farm access, turn right off the lane, following the public bridleway sign through a gate. Go through a second gate to a tri-directional

■ *The church at nearby West Grinstead where Belloc is buried* ■

sign and go left, following a public bridleway sign, ignoring the stile to your right. Cross two footbridges and swing right through a gate, following a public bridleway sign, continuing over a gate. Go over a field and through a gate to the lane.

9 Turn right on the lane back to the parking area.

Hilaire Belloc was an ardent Catholic and the focus of his devotions – the Catholic Shrine of Our Lady of Consolation & St Francis at nearby **West Grinstead** – is where he is buried in a family grave near the tower. The church can be accessed off the A272. Go back to the A272 and turn right. Cross the A24 junction and proceed for just over a mile, turning right down Park Lane. Drive on for a further mile to the church at the junction.

7 Loxwood

Wey Marked

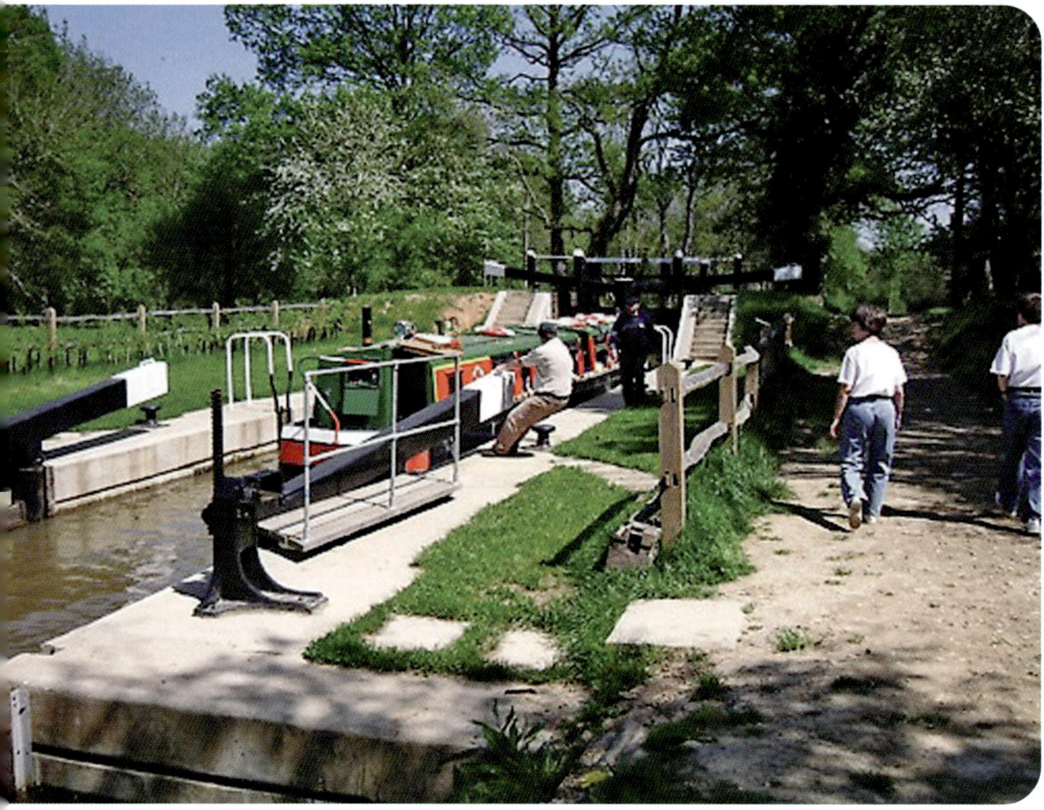

■ *The Wey and Arun Canal* ■

Beginning in the village of Loxwood, our serpentine route along an old towpath, follows the curves of the newly-restored Wey and Arun Canal, a waterway now given over to coots, anglers and pleasure craft, with the 50 ft converted narrowboat, the *Zachariah Keppel*, taking passengers on the most languid of excursions into the Sussex countryside. The canal was originally opened at Loxwood in 1816 with the high ambition of transporting a payload of 130,000 tons each year. However, incoming seaweed and lime for use as agricultural fertilisers and coal and gravel, together with outgoing farm produce making up the bulk of cargoes, never

> **GRADE: 2**
> **ESTIMATED CALORIE BURN: 565**
>
> **Description:** A canal, lanes and woodlands amble with an opportunity to pace yourself alongside the 2 mph *Zachariah Keppel*.
> **Distance:** 3¾ miles.
> **Time:** 2 hours.
> **Gradient:** Slight inclines only. No stiles.
> **Underfoot:** The majority of the walk uses a flat canal towpath and rural tracks and lanes. The woodland sections are also easy. But beware the imposing but highly unpleasant giant hogweed encountered at Point 8 of the walk. It should not be touched as its sap causes skin irritation and blistering.
> **Starting point:** Park in Loxwood, east of the junction of Loxwood Road and the B2133, on Farm Close opposite Loxwood Surgery. GR 041315.
> **How to get there:** Loxwood is around 4 miles north-west of Billingshurst. Turn north off the A272 on the B2133 to Loxwood.
> **OS map:** Explorer 134 Crawley & Horsham.
> **Refreshments:** On the route, the excellent Onslow Arms caters for all canal users and the pub is the base of the Wey and Arun Canal Trust, all cruises setting off from its slipway. Saturday, Sunday and public holiday cruises begin at the end of March and extend until the autumn. Booking is recommended. Telephone: 01403 752403.

exceeded 18,000 tons. This poor tonnage, coupled with the coming of the railways, signalled the end of the canal and it was closed in 1888.

But gloriously, over a hundred years on, the embarking whistle sounds and, matching the narrowboat for speed, we pass rebuilt bridges, locks, slipways and winding holes (explanatory leaflets are helpfully provided by the Wey and Arun Canal Trust at convenient locations). The path loops eastwards to a newly-constructed aqueduct and a short stretch on a quiet country lane. The final section of the walk visits woodland and a decaying old mill, the ancient structure hopefully making the Trust's list for renewal.

1 Go to the end of **Farm Close**, swinging right by the **Loxwood Surgery**, and take the signed footpath left to the lane.

2 Turn left using the footway and continue to the **Onslow Arms**, going left along the towpath. Pass the locks and the winding hole and walk on to the aqueduct, following the signposts to **Drungewick Lane**.

3 Turn right along the lane and pass the entrance to **Drungewick Manor**, continuing for one third of a mile.

4 Turn right, following a public bridleway sign, passing **Drungewick Kennels**, going through a gate. Swing left on a tree-lined path between fields, walking on at the bridleway sign and going left into a wood. Keep forward at the next bridleway signs to the next set of four signs.

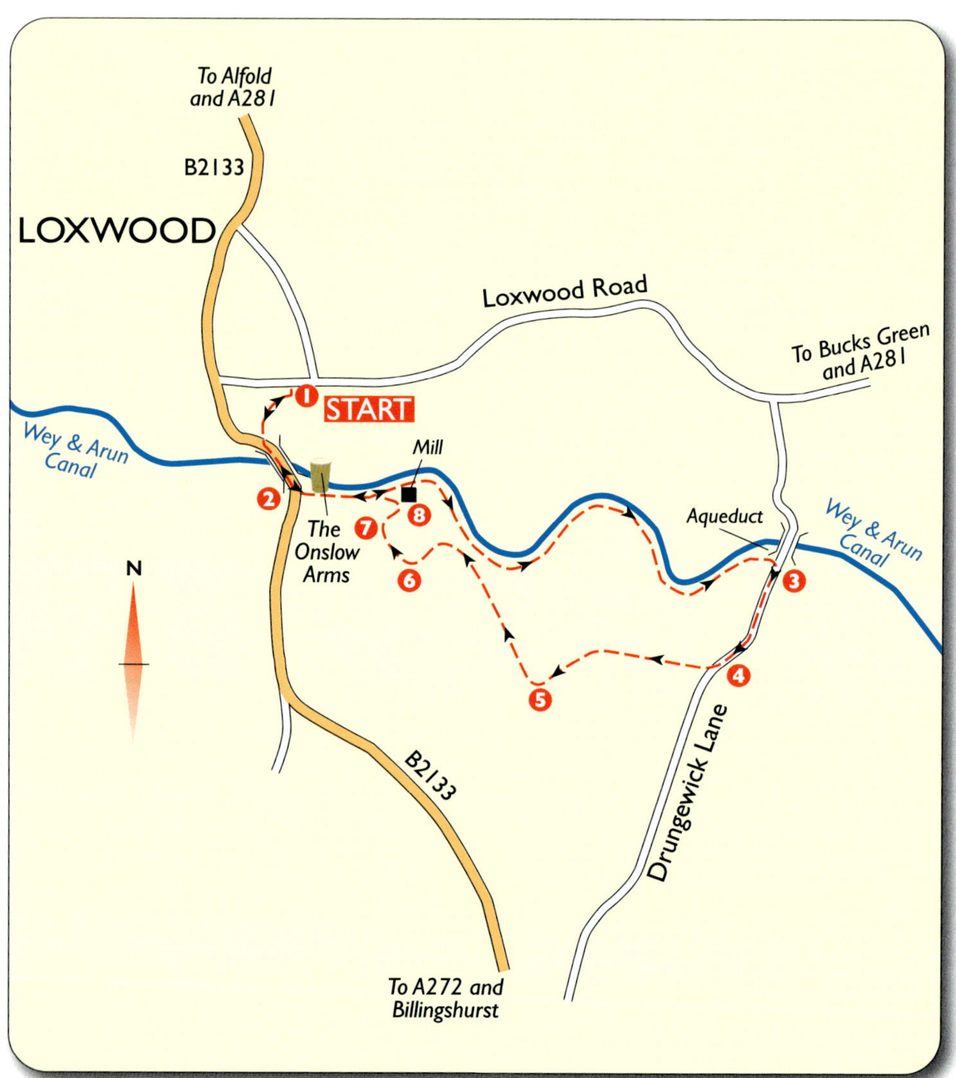

■ *The canal is a serene spot for cruising* ■

5 Turn right, following the public footpath sign in the wood, and go left at the next footpath sign downhill, following the footpath sign right. Go left at the next sign over a footbridge and swing left through a gate and leave the wood. Continue between a hedge and a fence and swing left between the chestnut fencing to a gate.

6 Go through the gate and turn right on the lane, following the public footpath sign, and veer right.

7 Turn right on the lane, following the public bridleway sign, passing **Hurst Cottage** and continuing to the mill.

8 Turn left by the mill, following the public footpath sign. Cross the bridges and swing right across the meadow to the canal. Turn left on the outward route back to the start.

8 Fulking
Satanic Traverses

■ *Looking south towards Devil's Dyke* ■

This spirited assault on a rearing flank of the South Downs conquers a viewpoint whose acclivity is attributable to the Devil. In a fit of pique, he is supposed to have abandoned his attempt at scooping out a ditch to the sea and flung down the earth in contempt. Bravo old forktail! You have created a hill offering some of the best views in England, described by the famous landscape painter John Constable as 'the finest in the world'.

Our route follows a winding path from the pretty village of Fulking, with its beautifully preserved fountain heads, to the top of Devil's Dyke, a popular beauty spot smothered with wild flowers during spring and summer. At the

GRADE: 2
ESTIMATED CALORIE BURN: 700

Description: A 'straight at him' 500 ft climb of the Devil's Dyke, returning downhill through woodland to the village of Poynings, the last leg over seasonally flower-brimmed meadows accompanying two streams.

Distance: 4 miles.

Time: 2½ hours.

Gradient: 15% of the route – nearly all of Point 1. Fourteen stiles.

Underfoot: Undulating grit and turf tracks and field and streamside paths, some of which can be muddy after rain.

Starting point: Park on The Street in Fulking or (if intending to patronise the pub) in the Shepherd and Dog car park at the western end of the village. GR 248116.

How to get there: Fulking is easily accessed off the A23 – the Brighton to London road. Some 3 miles north of the A23/A27 junction, turn westwards on the A281 and continue, keeping forward at the bend, following the signposts to Poynings. Continue for just over a mile to Fulking.

OS map: Explorer 122 Brighton & Hove.

Refreshments: On the route is the wonderfully situated Shepherd and Dog in Fulking – its streamside garden is a delight – serving good bar meals. The upmarket Royal Oak in Poynings offers a sophisticated bistro-type menu with daily specials. At the summit of Devil's Dyke is a pub of the same name providing standard bar meals.

summit are three illustrated topography boards that identify distant landmarks, including the highest hill in Kent, Ashdown Forest and the Isle of Wight, some 46 miles to the south-west. There is also a talking telescope. The homeward section through National Trust woodland passes through the equally attractive village of Poynings, before returning over farmland and by pretty streamside paths to Fulking.

1 Walk west through the village downhill past the **Stammers Hill** sign to the bend and go left by the **Shepherd and Dog**, following the blue arrow marker. Walk on for 50 yards and go right up the steps, following the yellow arrow marker on a path between the field edge and the hedge. Swing right to the stile and cross left up the steps, entering the National Trust's **Fulking Escarpment**. Climb up on the broad track, swinging left and right to the direction post and the tracks junction. Go forward, ignoring the tracks to the left and right, and swing left in an arc and then veer right on a broad green track. Go through a gate near the summit and left, following a yellow arrow marker, and continue through a gate to the left of the **Devil's Dyke pub** and on to the topography boards to the left of the car park.

2 Walk on, keeping to the dyke ridge path, and continue to a second stile, crossing to the left in the direction of **Poynings church tower**. Steer right, following the yellow arrow marker, for 250 yards, heading for the farm buildings in the mid distance.

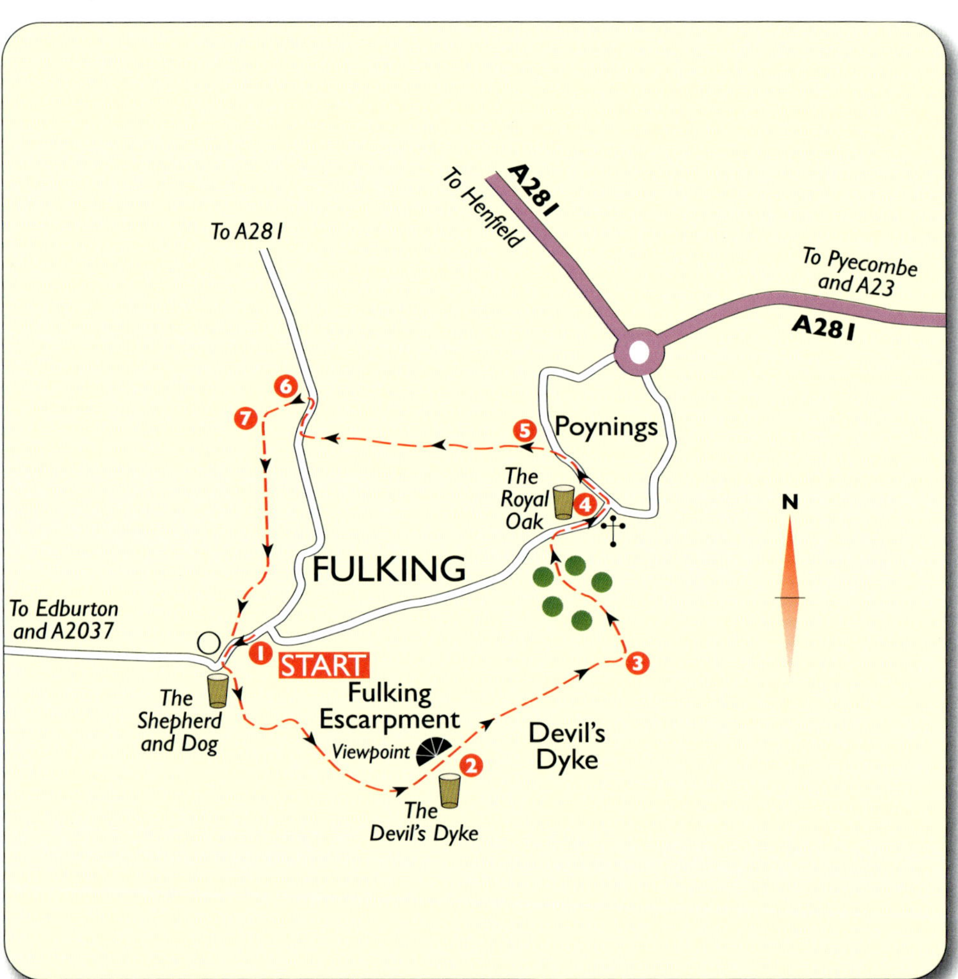

The fountain head in Fulking

3 Go left on a track downhill and through a gate, dropping into a wood. Keep straight forward at the No 4 arrow marker and swing right at the wood edge, passing the **Devil's Dyke** sign. Emerge on **Dyke Lane** into **Poynings** and turn right to the **Royal Oak**.

4 Go left (footpath sign on the pub garden wall), swinging left and right to a gate. Go through and right to a second gate and cross a stream and go left, following a public footpath sign, to a lane.

5 Go left, passing **Mill House** and the treatment works, and cross a third stile, following a yellow arrow marker and a stream to another yellow arrow marker and go left away from the stream over a field. Cross a fourth stile, following the yellow arrow marker, and cross a fifth stile, keeping forward and veering left to a gate. Cross a sixth stile to a lane and go right, swinging left by **Knole House**.

6 Cross a stream and immediately go left, following a public footpath sign, for 15 yards and go left again over a seventh stile, following a footpath sign alongside the stream. Cross a footbridge and continue forward to a second and more substantial footbridge.

7 Go left over the footbridge, following the public footpath sign, crossing an eighth stile and walking on over a field to cross a ninth stile and a planked bridge. Cross a tenth stile and continue hedgeside, crossing an eleventh and a twelfth stile and a track. Keep forward across a thirteenth stile and cross a fourteenth stile in the field corner, going right through a kissing gate. Continue for 120 yards and go left, following a footpath sign across a field, swinging left to a kissing gate. Go through left, following a footpath sign into **Fulking**.

9 *Milland*

Entrusted Trees

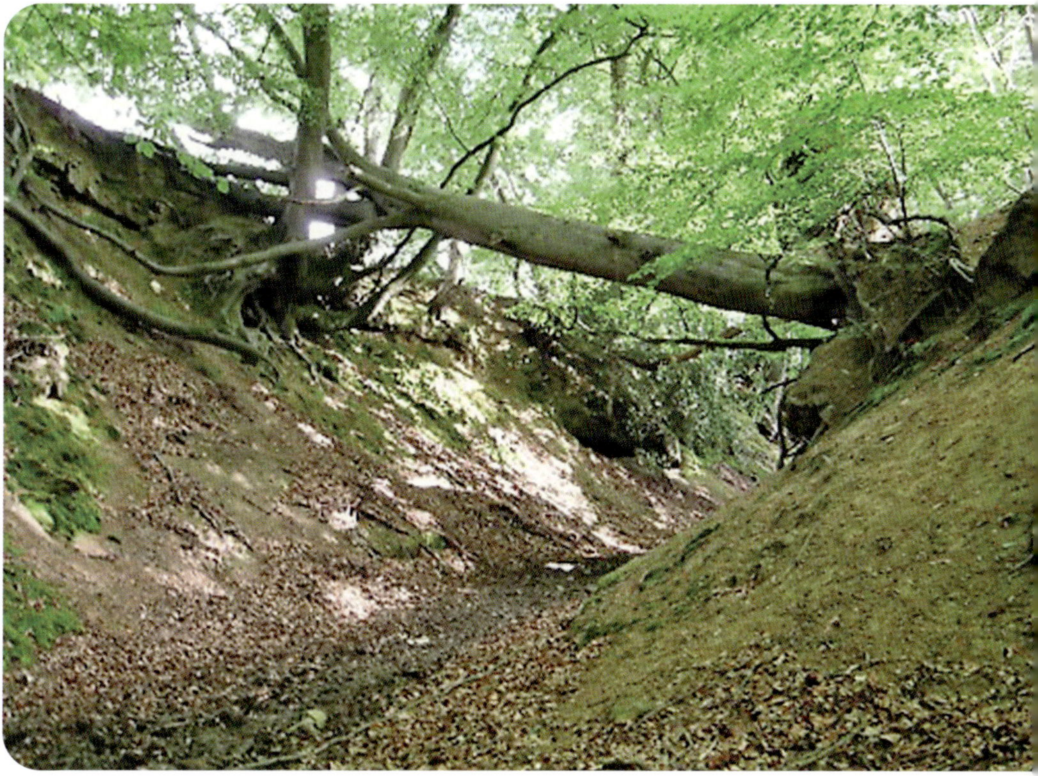

■ *Some of the paths on this walk are enchanted* ■

Many of the rare woodlands of West Sussex were once off limits to walkers but, in these more enlightened times, open access policies embraced by the Forestry Commission have opened up large tracts of land for us all to enjoy. Using part of the Border Path this leafy, energising walk through hundreds of acres of preserved and cared for forest in three locations provides exercise and repose in perfect measure.

The winding way uses a centuries-old sunken trackway hidden by gnarled roots and boughs, leading through former private estates to a modern church and the 11th-century Tuxlith chapel in the care of the Friends of Friendless Churches. A wide variety of trees will be encountered, including

> **GRADE: 2**
> **ESTIMATED CALORIE BURN: 630**
>
> **Description:** A sequestered woodland walk using paths and trackways leading to an old chapel.
> **Distance:** 4 miles.
> **Time:** 2½ hours.
> **Gradient:** There is one mildly taxing climb at Point 4.
> **Underfoot:** Some of the bridleways may be hoof marked and muddy after wet weather.
> **Starting point:** Park in the car park of the Black Fox Inn (if a customer) or in the lay-by opposite. GR 830291.
> **How to get there:** Milland is around 6 miles north-west of Midhurst on a minor road. Turn northwards off the A272 and go through Iping, continuing to Milland. The parking area is a further 1½ miles north-west of Milland – turn left on the B2070 for 250 yards to the lay-by opposite the Black Fox Inn.
> **OS map:** Explorer 133 Haslemere & Petersfield.
> **Refreshments:** Opposite the start of the walk, the Black Fox Inn offers both bar and restaurant meals.

sweet chestnut whose nuts can be gathered in autumn. In places between the boughs are swathes of rhododendrons, their electric pinks illuminating the glades in May and June. The presence of such once widely fashionable exotics reminds us of the arboreal extravagance of great houses like Milland Place whose now impoverished walled garden may be glimpsed en route.

1 Walk back from the parking area, going north-east to the **Milland/Iping** junction sign and keep forward on the lane. Cross **Milland Lane** and keep forward, following the **Sussex Border Path** sign. Pass through the golf course, keeping forward at the public bridleway sign. Go past the car park and walk on to the four-directional signpost.

2 Turn right, following the public footpath sign on a track between two gate pillars. Keep straight on at the fork and leave the access way at **Hatch House** and follow the blue arrow marker left on a sunken track. Swing right, following the public bridleway sign. At the next marker post, keep forward, dropping down, following the blue arrow marker, descending left on a deeply sunken track. Go down to meet a lane end.

3 Turn right on a path, following the **Hollycombe Estate** sign, and continue on the main track as it swings left. At the next fork, keep left and go forward to the bridleway signs, swinging right. Keep forward at the public bridleway signs, swinging right to the next public bridleway signs.

4 Turn right, following the sign, with the old **Milland Place** garden wall to your left and walk on uphill on a track to **Milland Lane**.

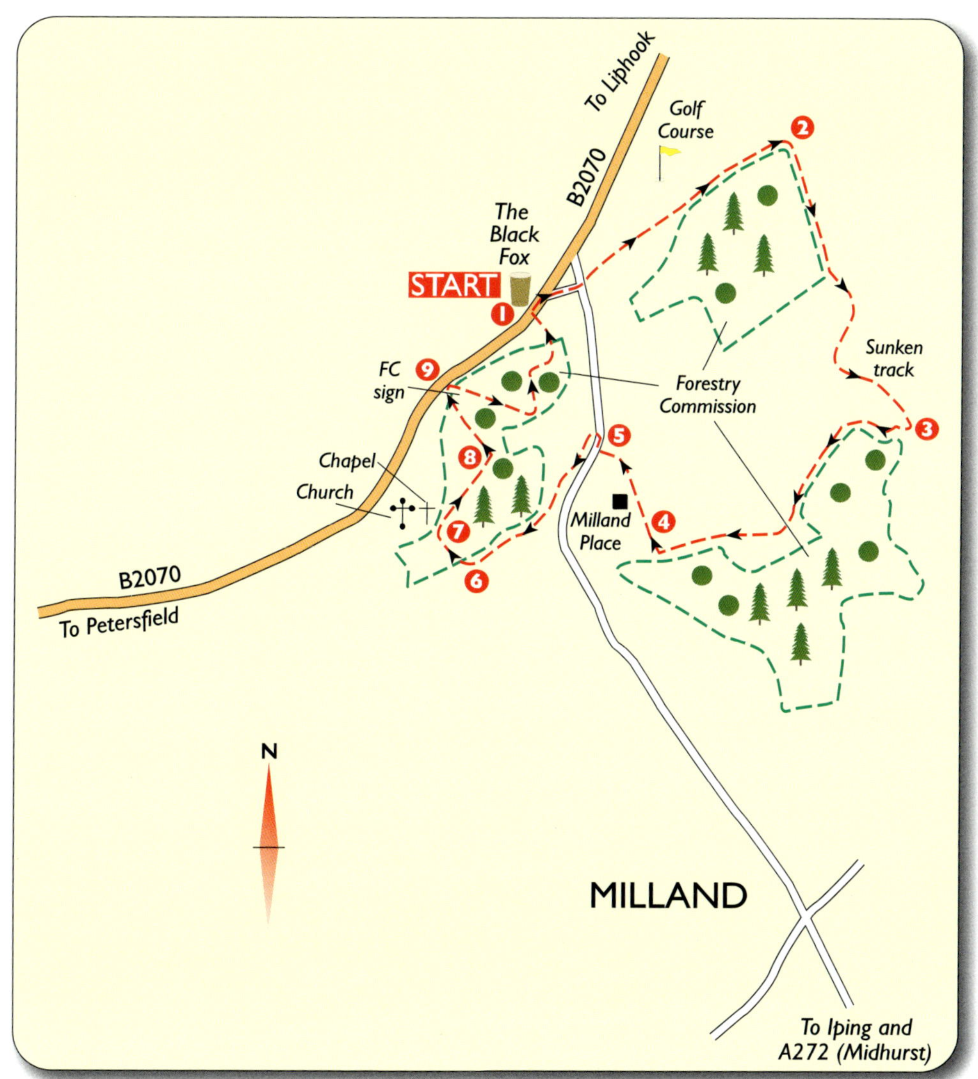

Rhododendrons flourish in some woodland clearings

5 Turn right on the lane and go left just past the post box, going left again, following the yellow arrow marker and a fence. Cross a stile, entering a wood, and keep forward, following the arrow marker in the clearing. Walk on to the signs.

6 Go right, following the arrow marker into the wood, and swing left to the lychgate. (If you want to visit, go through to the chapel and the church.)

7 Go right by the gate (ignoring the footpath signs) and follow the path by the chestnut fence. Walk on to a track.

8 Go left on the track and walk on towards the lane and Forestry Commission sign at the wood entrance.

9 Turn right on a track and follow it left. Swing right and left to the road and the **Black Fox Inn**.

10 Bignor

All Roads Lead to Rome

FOOTPATHS FOR FITNESS

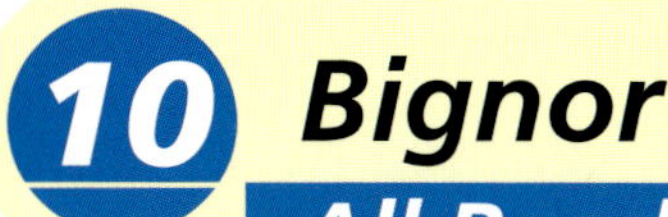

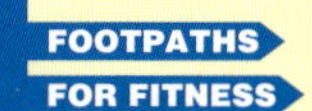

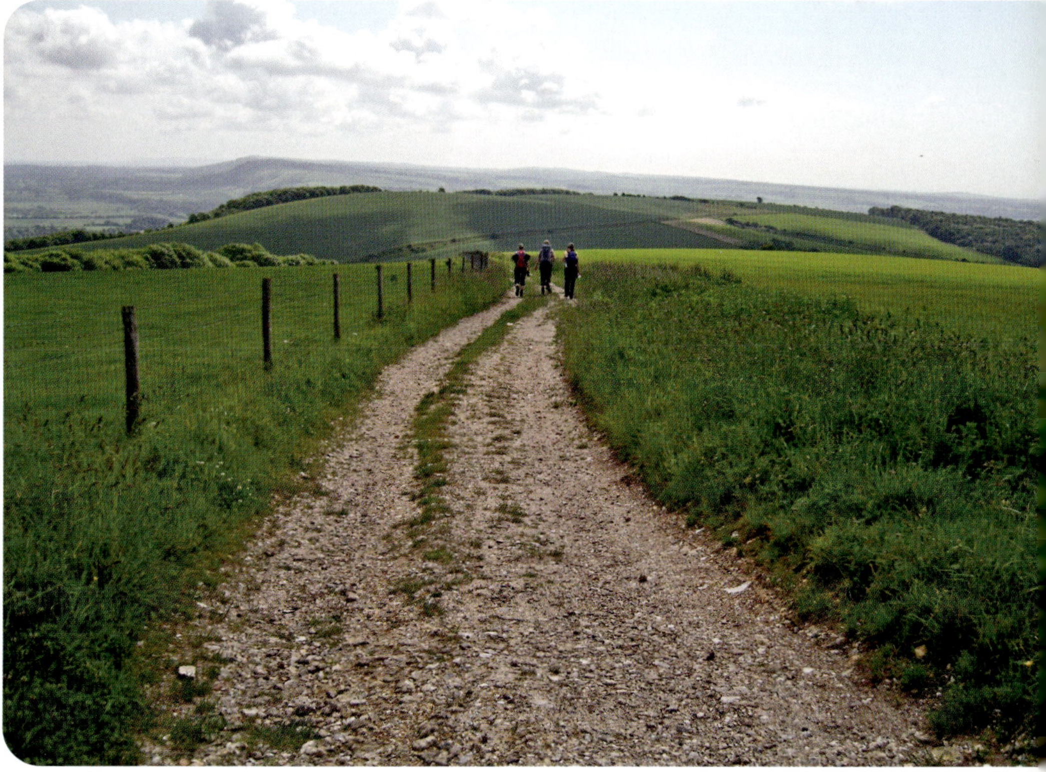

Walking on Westburton Hill

Around sixteen centuries have elapsed since the Romans abandoned these shores but their legacy remains strong hereabouts. The village of Bignor flies the eagle standard from the site of one of the best-preserved and most luxuriously appointed villas in England (it had sixty-five rooms and underfloor heating!) alongside a road – Stane Street – that was built to carry troops between Chichester (*Noviomagus Regensium*) and London (*Londinium*). Follow in the footsteps of the legionaries on a field path and ascend the steep Westburton and Bignor hills, passing the even older remains of Neolithic and Iron Age settlers who buried their dead on the heights.

GRADE: 2
ESTIMATED CALORIE BURN: 750

Description: Through an historic landscape of rolling hills and woodland, an exhilarating but quite demanding circuit using part of the South Downs Way, the walk also exploring the beautifully preserved Bignor village.
Distance: 4½ miles.
Time: 2½ hours.
Gradient: 30% of the route, climbing Westburton and Bignor hills at points 3,4 and 5. One stile.
Underfoot: The uplands tracks are well maintained; the woodland paths at the end of points 2 and 7 can be boggy after bad weather.
Starting point: The free car park at Bignor Roman villa. This fascinating site is open on Tuesday to Sunday and bank holidays between March and April. From May to October it is open daily. Telephone: 01798 869259. GR 987147.
How to get there: Bignor is about 6 miles north-west of Arundel off the A29. Approaching from the south, go left just after the Bury turn on West Burton Road. The Roman villa is signposted to the east of Bignor.
OS map: Explorer 121 Arundel & Pulborough.
Refreshments: Bignor Roman villa has a teashop and a picnic garden. When the villa is closed, the White Horse Inn, a five-minute drive north-west of Bignor, is a highly recommended stop.

The summit at nearly 700 ft commands terrific views to the south-west of the line of the famous road now utilised in part by the busy A285, a sweeping panorama of the sea also coming into view. The return path drops steeply down through woodland to return to the village. Overall, this is a fairly strenuous walk but the sense of accomplishment, the fitness benefits and the abiding sense of rambling through historical landscapes bring their rewards. Step out on the imperial road and remember the immortal words of fitness guru Julius Caesar – *veni*, *vidi*, *vici* – I came, I saw, I conquered!

1 Leave the **Roman villa** by the access road and walk on to the lane. Turn right for 200 yards.

2 Turn left off the lane, following a public footpath sign, going straight forward on a track over an arable field, heading for the field edge. At the edge, go left along the fence line. Cross a footbridge and swing right, following a public footpath sign. Cross a second bridge and swing left, following a yellow arrow marker. Swing left at the next signpost, passing a pond, and cross a planked bridge, following a stream down to a cottage.

3 Turn right, following a public footpath sign in front of the cottage, heading uphill on a winding track. At the fork, go left and keep climbing through woodland up **Westburton Hill**. Exit the wood at the public bridleway sign and keep forward.

4 Turn second right at the signposts on a track and go left uphill to the **South Downs Way** sign.

5 Turn right on a track, following the sign, and swing left, walking up to **Toby's Stone**. The memorial is inscribed with stirring words by Robert Louis Stevenson, honouring a former Master of the Cowdray Hunt. Continue forward on the track to the **Slindon Estate** signboard near the car park.

6 Turn right and right again on a lane, following the sign to the Roman villa, and drop down to the public footpath sign.

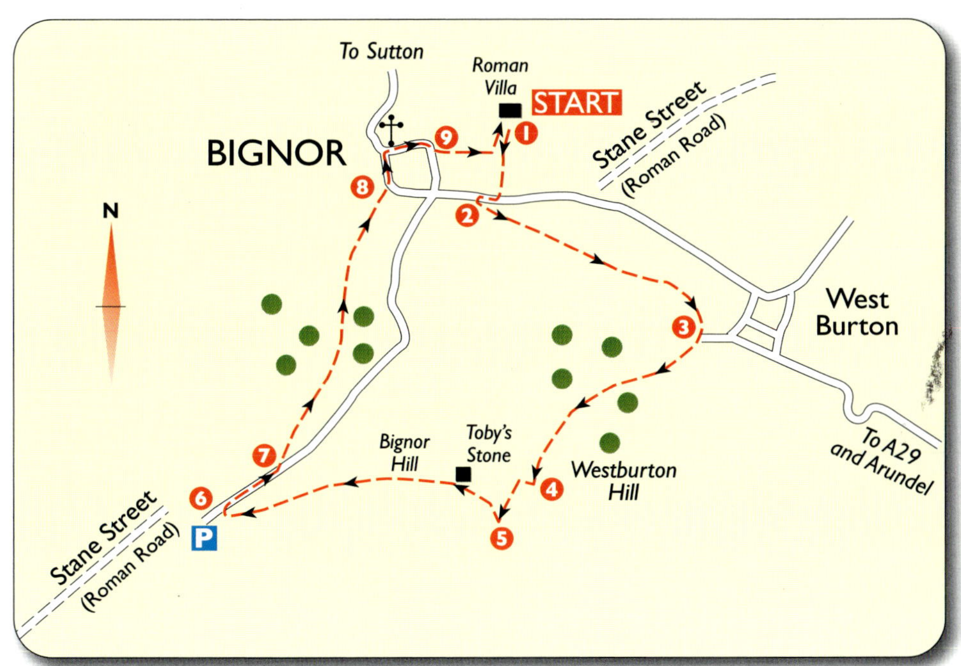

7 Go left off the lane, following the sign, through **Hanger Wood**. Drop down to the bench, swinging left and leaving the wood. Continue downwards on a field edge track. Cross a stile and follow the public footpath sign forward. Swing right at the field end and go forward to a track. Continue along the track to **Bignor**.

8 Turn left along the lane past **Malthouse Cottages** and walk on to the junction. Turn right opposite **Holy Cross church** and swing right round the bend to the **Yeoman's House**.

9 Turn left off the lane (signpost hidden in hedge) on a track and go through a kissing gate into a vineyard. Continue to the outward track from the Roman villa and turn left back to the parking area.

■ *The Yeoman's House in Bignor* ■

11 *West Stoke*

A Vespered Vale

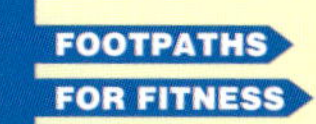

■ *The view from the Tansley Stone* ■

The **National Nature Reserve of Kingley Vale** occupies one of the most peaceful spots in the whole of West Sussex, sinuous, steep-sided hills embracing pastures and a 2,000-year-old yew grove – one of the largest in Europe. Resonating with the ghosts of ancient farmers who tended their flocks here and buried their dead on the summits, our short foray from the hamlet of West Stoke is as gentle and uplifting as a prayer.

The route orbits the vale on age-old tracks, passing earthworks, dykes and a sacred burial site – a collection of tumuli with fabulous views of Chichester Cathedral, Chichester Channel and the Isle of Wight to the south-west – the Devil's Humps. But oh no, sacrilege! His Satanic Majesty could never have put his name to these. Built at heaven's gate and once covered in mantles of glittering white chalk that could be seen for miles around, these mausoleums were the tombs of chieftains not devils. We must think again (see below*)!

GRADE: 2
ESTIMATED CALORIE BURN: 750

Description: Involving a steady climb of some 500 ft to an eminence that commands sweeping panoramas, this is a perimeters and field boundaries walk around a nature reserve, the high point visiting ancient burial sites – the English equivalent of the Valley of the Kings.
Distance: 4¾ miles.
Time: 2¾ hours.
Gradient: 15% of the route, at point 3. No stiles.
Underfoot: The path and tracks are largely flat and even.
Starting point: The National Nature Reserve free car park signposted off the bend 200 yards west of St Andrew's church in West Stoke. GR 825087.
How to get there: West Stoke is about 4 miles north-west of Chichester and is best accessed off the A286, turning off westwards at Mid Lavant and going through West Stoke to the parking area.
OS map: Explorer 120 Chichester.
Refreshments: On Sundays during the summer months, teas and snacks are available in West Stoke village hall, east of the church. Alternatively, the Fox and Hounds in Funtington, 2 miles west of West Stoke, is popular for bar meals.

Purchased for the nation in 1952, the reserve is now cared for by Natural England, its permanently open field museum at the entrance to the vale at the end of point 1 giving a wealth of information about the history of the area and its wildlife, which includes fallow and roe deer.

1   Turn right from the car park and follow the public footpath sign through a gate, going forward on a track. Continue to the signed entrance to **Kingley Vale National Nature Reserve** (the field museum is in front on your right). Go through a gate.

2   Turn left on a track, following the signpost, and walk on for 200 yards.

3   Turn right, following the public bridleway sign, on a steadily ascending track. Swing left away from the second of the **Kingley Vale National Nature Reserve** signs, following a blue arrow marker, and keep climbing up, steering right at the fork, following the blue arrow marker. Keep going forward at the next post and continue to the tri-directional sign.

4 Turn right, following the blue arrow marker, and walk on through woodland, emerging into open country, passing the **Devil's Humps** (or the 'Chieftains' Chariots' – my renaming suggestion*) and the **Tansley Stone** – this commemorates Sir Arthur Tansley, the first chairman of the Nature Conservancy, the forerunner of English Nature and now known as Natural England. Follow the winding wooded track and continue to the direction signs and the next **Kingley Vale National Nature Reserve** sign.

5 Go right downhill on a track, following the public bridleway sign, at the edge of woodland. Leave the wood and keep descending to the direction post.

6 Go right, following the blue arrow marker, on a track between fields, returning to the end of point 1.

7 Go left on the outward route back to the start.

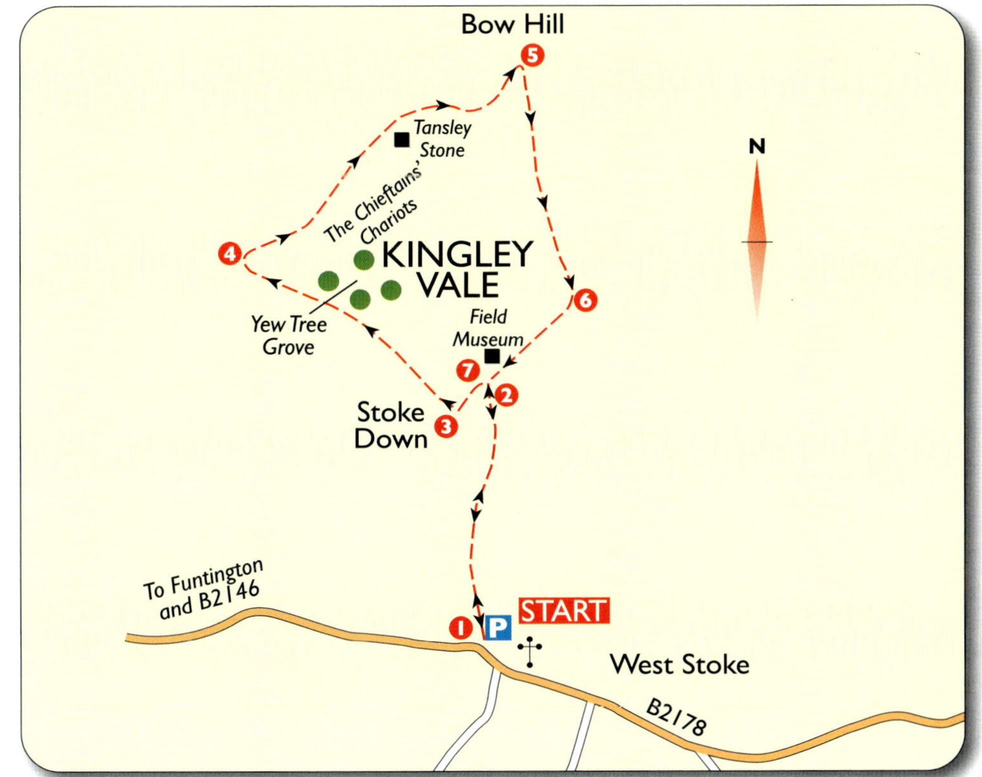

■ *The Stoughton memorial at West Stoke* ■

Before leaving sleepy **West Stoke**, you may care to visit its 11th-century **St Andrew's church**. It has two ecclesiastical marvels: a recently uncovered fragment of a wall painting dated between 1190 and 1220 and the Stoughton Memorial of 1635. The memorial depicts Lord of the Manor Adrian Stoughton kneeling opposite his wife Mary. At their feet are their children who hold the skulls of brothers and sisters who died in infancy.

When summer hordes retreat to cheery fire glow,
When autumnal wind incites the dormant winter's ire,
When recumbent nature cowers to slanted rain, to cold and seeping mire,
It's then the stout-hearted tramp aspires,
To lofty peaks, to winding wooded trails,
That beckoned booted disciple to ascend the lonely heights,
The craggy glens, the quiet vales.

Len Markham: *The Stout-hearted Tramp –*
inspired by my first visit to Kingley Vale, in dank October.

12 Cox Green

South of the Border

![A fishing pond passed on the route]

■ *A fishing pond passed on the route* ■

Perched on the edge of the county, with fine views at the start of sister Surrey, our route sets out on the Sussex Border Path, with sylvan twists and turns. The track takes in fishing ponds and woodland resplendent with oak, ash and hazel before delivering us to the sleepy hamlet of Rowhook. Here, with magnetised boots, you will dreamily cross the threshold of the Chequers Inn, its ancient creaks and polish beckoning. The second part of the walk begins by following the line of Stane Street, the Roman road linking Chichester (*Noviomagus Regensium*) and London (*Londinium*), the path plunging into the extensive Roman Wood, bluebell-filled in spring. A variety of wildlife will be encountered on this fascinating walk. Enjoy the abundance of wild flowers and watch out for basking carp and ambitious heron in the ponds.

GRADE: 2
ESTIMATED CALORIE BURN: 730

Description: An intricate fields, leafy lanes and woodlands ramble taking in feature ponds and part of the line of a Roman road, with a halfway highlight – a wonderfully unaltered English inn.
Distance: 4¾ miles.
Time: 2½ hours.
Gradient: Gentle ascents only in point 8 and the latter half of 12. Twelve stiles.
Underfoot: Parts of the wooded bridleways, particularly in Roman Wood at point 12, can become hoof churned following wet weather.
Starting point: Park off the bend on Baynards Lane at the northern end of the village, around the green triangle near the West Sussex county sign. GR 093349.
How to get there: Cox Green is around 4 miles north-west of Horsham off the A281, going north on the B2128 at Watts Corner.
OS map: Explorer 134 Crawley & Horsham.
Refreshments: The Chequers Inn on the route in Rowhook is popular for bar meals.

1 Walk south back into the village, passing the West Sussex sign, using the footway, and pass **Jasmine House**.

2 Go left, following a public footpath sign over a stile. Cross a second stile into a paddock and veer left, crossing a third stile. Cross a planked bridge and continue hedgeside to the field corner and cross a fourth stile.

3 Turn left on a quiet lane and walk up to the Sussex Border Path sign adjacent to **Godleys**.

4 Keep straight forward, following the **Sussex Border Path**, crossing a fifth stile. Continue alongside the mesh fence. In the field corner, go left, following the Sussex Border Path sign, on a concrete access lane and continue to the public footpath signs near the disused cattle grid. Keep forward, ignoring the public footpath sign to the left, and continue for 250 yards.

5 Turn right off the **Sussex Border Path**, following a public footpath sign, and keep hedgeside, walking on to the field corner. Go left, following the

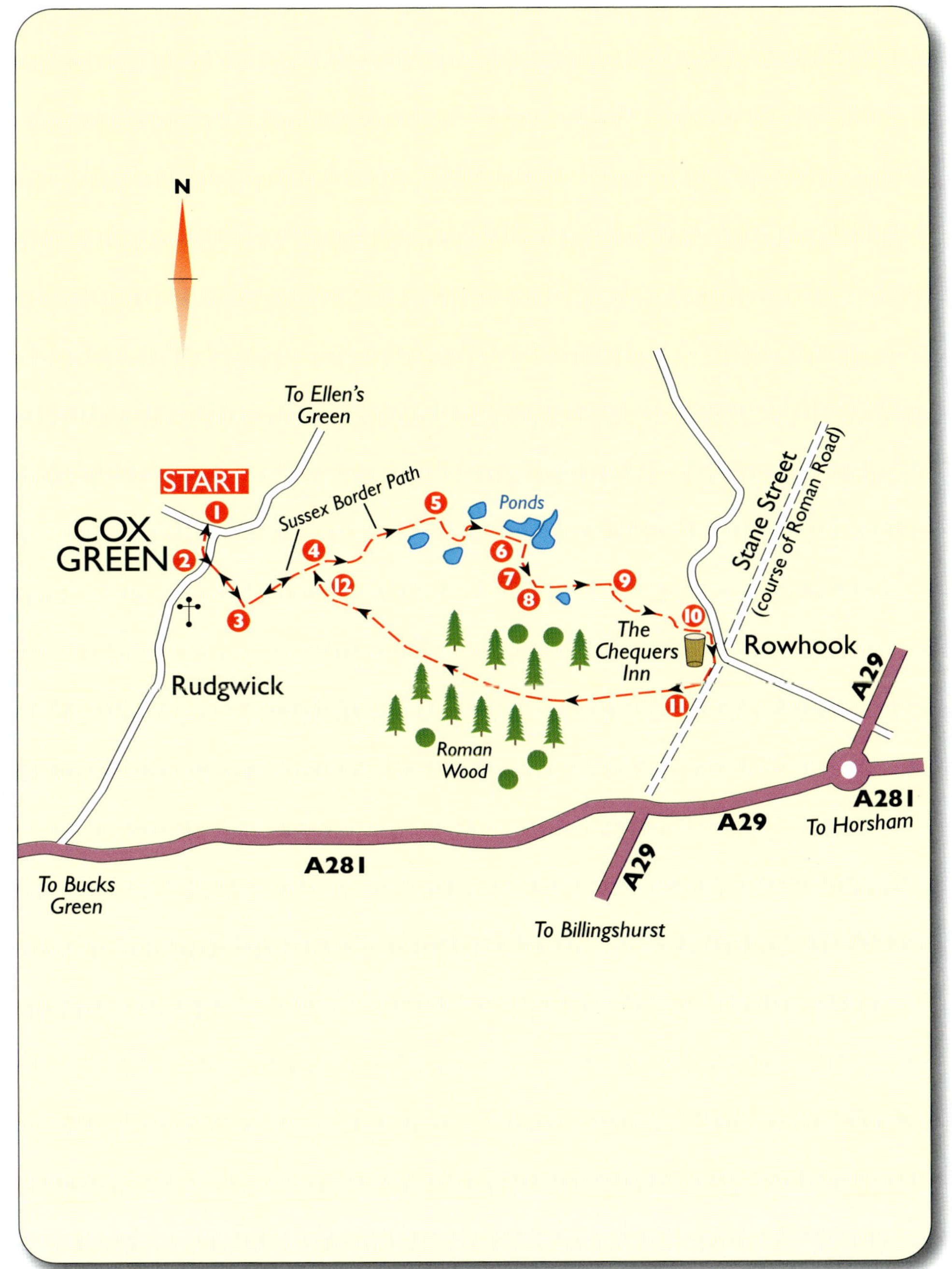

N
To Ellen's Green
START
1
COX GREEN
2
Sussex Border Path
4
5
Ponds
6
7
8
9
3
12
10
The Chequers Inn
Rowhook
Stane Street (course of Roman Road)
11
Rudgwick
Roman Wood
A29
A281
A29
A281
To Horsham
To Bucks Green
To Billingshurst

public footpath sign hedgeside downhill, swinging left by the pond in the bottom. Go right, following a public footpath sign through a gate, entering a copse. Cross an access lane and keep forward at the next set of signs, following the public footpath sign at the side of the pond. Follow the next sign forward to the larger pond.

6 Turn right at the dam wall between the two ponds on a track and continue to the left of a gate.

7 Go through the gate right and turn immediately left, following a public footpath sign at the field edge, continuing for 200 yards.

8 Go left, following a public footpath sign. Cross a sixth stile into a wood and take a track down left. Go right at the public footpath sign over a footbridge and weave up left. Cross a seventh stile, following a public footpath sign, dropping down alongside the wood edge and a fence. Where the ditch ends, keep forward and climb up, keeping left of the pond. Continue to the

■ *Burnt House, near Roman Wood* ■

public footpath sign in the field corner. Keep forward, passing a second smaller pond, and go right in the next field corner, following a public footpath sign, heading for the sign in the middle of a field.

9 Turn left at the sign, veering right across the field, passing **Millfield House** to the left. Cross the footbridge and keep left hedgeside to the next public footpath sign in the corner. Go right for 130 yards and then go left, following a public footpath sign fenceside, crossing an eighth stile in the corner to **Rowhook Road**.

10 Turn right using the wide verge alongside the road, passing the **Chequers Inn**, and turn immediately right on the lane – the old course of **Stane Street**. Pass **Stane Cottage** and walk on to the **Waterlands** sign.

■ *Dog roses* ■

11 Turn right off the lane, following a public bridleway sign (obscured by trees to the left), and go through the gateway of **Burnt House**, keeping forward with the house to the left, to the signs. Continue at the public bridleway signs, keeping forward. Go ahead at the next sign, swinging right and left. Cross the track and keep forward (ignore the 'Please Keep Out' signs which refer to equestrian access) and follow the white-tipped posts downhill, crossing a footbridge. Keep forward at the bridleway sign, walking up to a gate. Go to the right of the gate, following a public bridleway sign, swinging right and up across a large field. At the field edge, swing right, following a public bridleway sign, passing **Little Coopers** on a concrete access way and continue to the Sussex Border Path sign.

12 Keep forward, swinging right, and continue to **Godleys**, turning left on the outward route back to the start.

13 *Slindon*

Around Belloc's Boyhood Home

■ *The Folly, at point 3 of the circuit* ■

The great author and poet Hilaire Belloc came to Slindon as a boy in 1877. His soul has never left the beautiful landscape that, time and again, inspired his prodigious pen, waxing eternal. His beloved woods and hills now overlook a showpiece village and parkland largely under the care of the National Trust. Drawn north from Slindon by a skyline

GRADE: 2
ESTIMATED CALORIE BURN: 770

Description: A hilltop and woods ramble with some long-distance views.
Distance: 4¾ miles.
Time: 2¾ hours.
Gradient: 20% of the route – at points 2 and 3. Two stiles.
Underfoot: Distinct and well maintained footpaths and tracks for most of the way although the track at the start of point 2 may be muddy after heavy rain.
Starting point: Park alongside the lane opposite St Richard's Catholic church. GR 962085.
How to get there: Slindon is around 5 miles north-west of Arundel off the A27 and the A29.
OS map: Explorer 121 Arundel & Pulborough.
Refreshments: There are no refreshment facilities along the route (Slindon village pub is now closed) but the open ground in the shadow of The Folly at the end of point 3 is ideal for picnics.

18th-century mock castle, this lovely walk offers peace, solitude and shade in abundance in the hilltop Nore Wood, the return route taking us through the popular Slindon Wood, passing Park Pale, a ring of ancient earthworks constructed to retain an enclosure for deer. Back in the village, we pass a delightful pond and Belloc's former home and, as a fitting finale, we discover a church treasure unique in Sussex.

1 Go left on the lane, passing **Slindon College**, and swing right and left, passing the village sign. Go left up the bank to find a footpath and weave down, walking on to a point opposite the T-junction near the school sign. Go right at the junction, dropping down the lane left to **Courthill Farm**.

2 Go left off the lane on a track, following a public footpath sign. Go through a gate and climb up to a point 100 yards short of a barn.

3 Turn right off the track, following the yellow arrow marker by a redundant stile to the left of a reservoir. Cross two stiles right and walk on uphill on a field edge path parallel to the track to your left. Continue fieldside, going left, following the public footpath sign to **The Folly** and a triangulation pillar. Turn right on the track and walk on to a gate to your left.

4 Turn left off the track (footpath pointer missing) into **Nore Wood**. Keep forward on the woodland track (reservoir left) and follow the yellow arrow marker on a post right. Walk on to the timber barrier across the track, swinging right, following the yellow arrow marker. Swing left by the pheasant feeder and go left at the fork by the big beech, following the blue arrow marker, swinging left and right. Follow the path as it snakes left downhill and swing right, dropping height. Pass the signpost to **Eartham** and keep forward, walking on forward, following the blue arrow markers to the National Trust sign and the lane.

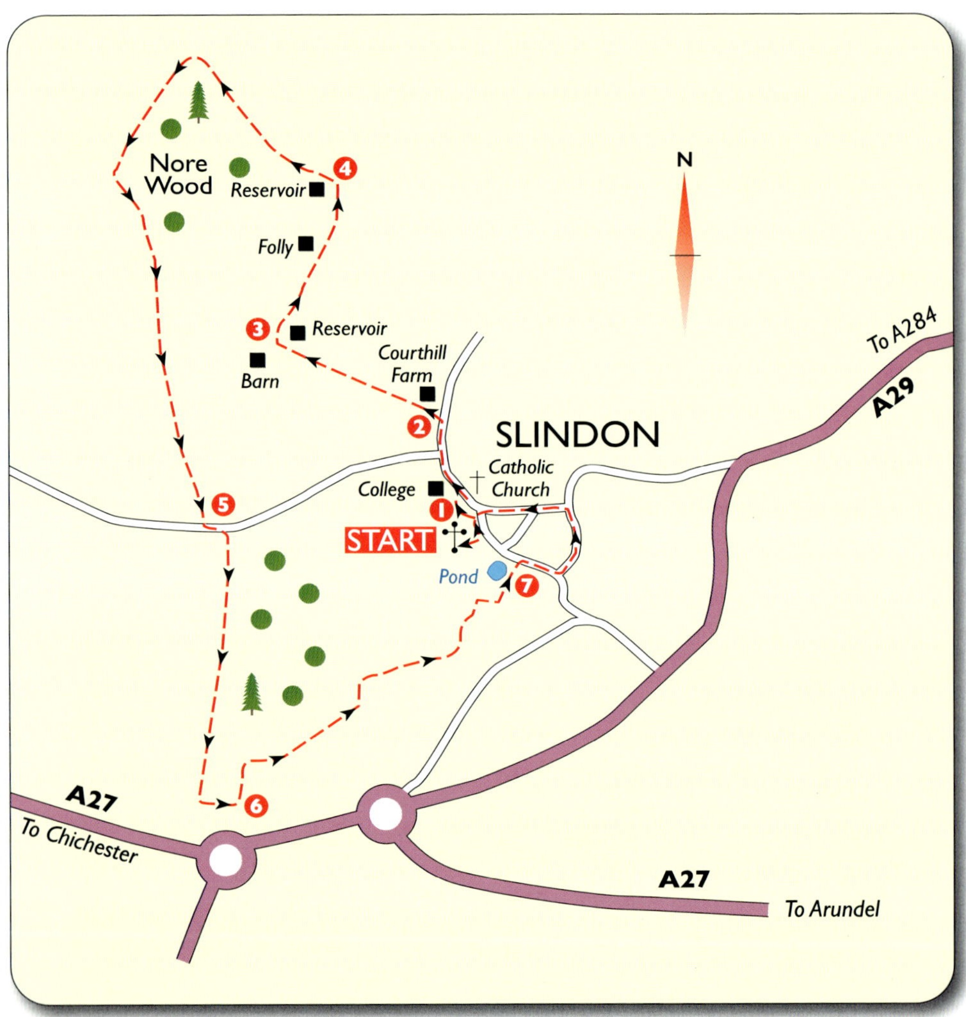

■ *The blue plaque outside Belloc's former home* ■

5 Cross the lane and fork left, following the blue arrow marker. Swing right on **Slindon Bottom Road** (little traffic – access only), walking on to the junction. Turn left on the lane for 250 yards.

6 Go left off the lane over the parking area, forking right through a gap between a fence and a gate. At the fork, steer right on a stony track uphill. At the next fork, swing left and right and go next left. At the broad track in front of **Park Pale**, go right and at the fork, keep left. Go next left through a breach in the pale and walk on to a red gate. Keep forward, swinging right and left. At the next fork, go left with the field to your left, walking up towards the college, and swing right away from the playing fields, going left at the **Slindon Estate** sign to a pond. Swing right by the pond to the lane.

7 Turn right along the lane and walk on to the junction. Go left on the lane using the footway and swing left, passing **Bleak House**; marked with a blue plaque, this was the home of Hilaire Belloc. Continue towards the starting point and turn left down **Church Hill** to visit the 12th-century **church of St Mary**. Its most prized possession is an effigy unique in Sussex. Carved in oak beneath a protective iron cage, it depicts Anthony St Leger in the armour of the Wars of the Roses. The knight died in 1539, the patination of thousands of caressing fingers (including, no doubt, the young Belloc) giving the figure a rare sheen.

Turn left and left again back to the starting point.

■ *Anthony St Leger* ■

Guildenhurst

London's Lost Route to the Sea

■ The Flood Gate Bridge crossed on the walk ■

This delightful waterside ramble follows part of the Wey-South Path, the route companioning the lazy curves of a canal that once linked the wharves of London with the English Channel but was closed in 1888. You can almost hear the chug-chug of the *Sussex Pride* and smell her master's pipe as you follow bends, sweet with reeds, wild flowers and birdsong, to Lording's Lock and beyond, where a remarkable canal revival by a team of volunteers is underway. Here you will see a restored waterwheel, the only one of its type on the canal system, the still empty aqueduct and lock chamber awaiting further work. Accompanying the canal, the path crosses the superbly rebuilt Flood Gate Bridge before climbing to farmland where you will enjoy panoramic views of the Arun and distant villages, the return route following water meadow tracks and the shoreline of a beautiful lake.

Part of the local canal system north of Guildenhurst has already been revitalised and public cruises can be enjoyed from Loxwood – see Walk 7.

GRADE: 2
ESTIMATED CALORIE BURN: 770

Description: A fairly long but totally peaceful and absorbing route by river and canal, the inspirational restoration works, including a waterwheel, a bridge and a fine example of the hedgelayer's craft, making you want to grab a shovel!
Distance: 4¾ miles.
Time: 3 hours.
Gradient: Fairly flat canal and riverside paths with one climb at point 5. Eight stiles.
Underfoot: Being low lying, some stretches are inevitably muddy and overgrown in places.
Starting point: The Limeburners has a car park for customers – please seek permission from the staff. Alternatively, you can leave your car alongside the B2133. GR 073254.
How to get there: Guildenhurst is 1 mile west of Billingshurst (A29) and east of Wisborough Green. From Billingshurst take the A272 and turn off south along the B2133 for 250 yards to the Limeburners.
OS map: Explorer 134 Crawley & Horsham.
Refreshments: The Limeburners serves good bar meals, including fresh fish, and has a pleasant beer garden. There are picnic tables at Lording's Lock and alongside the Flood Gate Bridge at point 4.

1 Go left from the inn for 150 yards and turn right along the lane signed '**Guildenhurst Manor**'. Walk forward almost to the manor entrance drive.

2 Turn right over a stile, following a footpath sign, and cross a meadow right to a second stile left of a gate. Cross and walk over the next meadow to a third stile and cross, going right, following a signpost downhill to a bridge over the canal. Cross.

3 Go left and keep forward to a fourth stile. Cross and keep forward to a large field.

4 Go right hedgeside, heading away from the canal. Swing right at the end of the field then swing left to find a hidden signpost and cross a fifth stile, going right to the **Lording's Lock** restoration. Keep forward, crossing the footbridge, and go through the kissing gate, following the yellow arrow marker and the footpath right. After 80 yards, go right through a kissing gate, following a yellow arrow marker. Swing left on the canal bank, cross a wooden bridge and go down steps. Cross a second bridge right and keep forward, going through a kissing gate, following the yellow arrow marker. Go right over **Flood Gate Bridge** – restored 2002 – following the public footpath sign and go left on the bank – note the exquisite, newly laid hedge to your right – and cross a sixth stile, keeping forward, following the public footpath sign.

5 At the next signs, cross a seventh stile and go through a gate left on an ascending farm track. Go left by **Lee Place Farm** at the top on the access drive. Follow the drive right to the entrance and go through a gate to the four-directions sign.

6 Go sharp left, following the public bridleway sign, on a track between a hedge and a fence. At the **Frithwood Farm** entrance, go immediately right, following a public bridleway sign hedgeside into a field. Go through gates

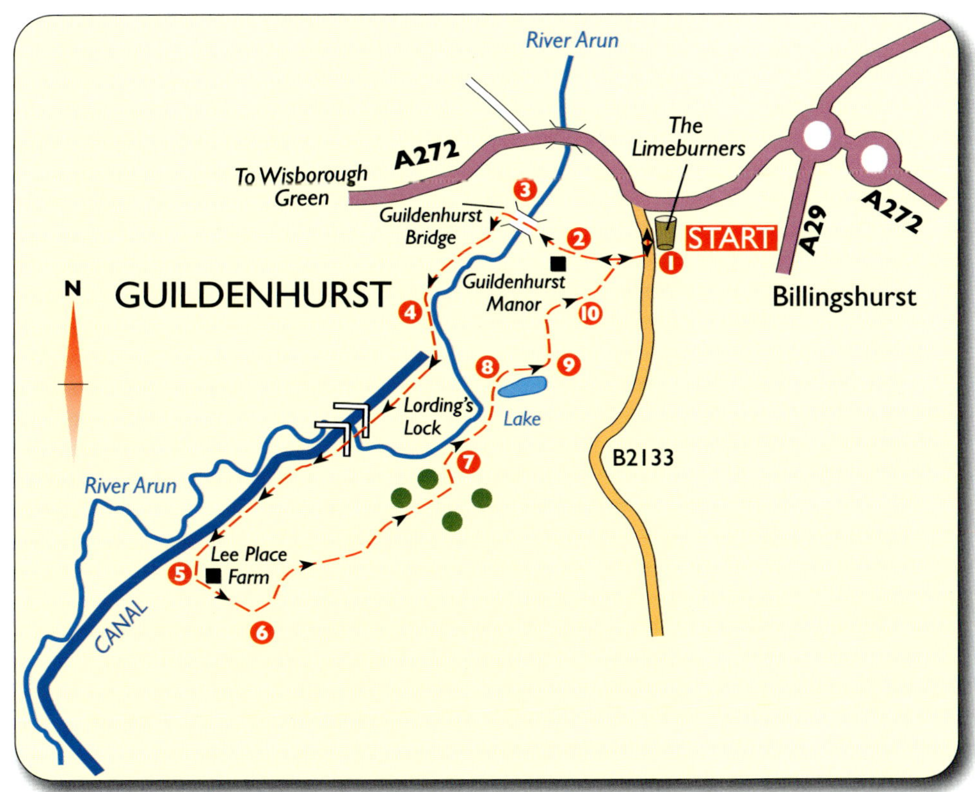

■ *A layered hedge near the canal* ■

into the second and third fields and swing left to a gate. Go through into a fourth field and head left for a gap between the two woods. Where the path bifurcates, fork right uphill over the meadow, heading left for the top of the field. With the sign 100 yards ahead, go left on a raised track at the field/wood edge for about 200 yards to a public footpath sign.

7 Go right downhill through a copse to the river. Go right. Cross an eighth stile and follow the riverbank. Go left over the footbridge.

8 Turn right by the lake, following the footpath sign to the boathouse.

9 Turn left uphill and keep left of the big barn. Go left at the marker post by the next barn and go right, following the signs over a planked bridge. Walk on by the side of a railed fence and go right at the corner to the next corner.

10 Go left, following the signs, and (ignoring the broad track right) keep straight forward, going through a small gate and heading diagonally right across a field. Go through a gate and forward to a kissing gate, going through and right, back onto the outward route to return to the start.

South Stoke

On the Trail of the Pride of Sussex

■ *The view from the Black Rabbit pub* ■

Properly accoutred for this walk, you would dress as a knight, your cavalcade flying the royal standard, as our path follows the aptly-named Monarchs Way. King Charles II retreated to exile in France along our route after his defeat at the Battle of Worcester in 1651. This historic, topographically varied and wonderfully energising walk begins in the sleepy riverside village of South Stoke, the path accompanying a lazy loop of the River Arun before heading south into a park created by the 11th Duke of Norfolk in 1789 as a playground for his imposing castle. And here you may find a more reclusive treasure, our county flower, the round-headed rampion, the Pride of Sussex – a mop headed little blue rarity that blooms in summer – hiding amongst the field margins.

Leaving the glides of the River Arun we climb steeply to enjoy sovereign views from the park east, north and south, the track discovering a lake skimmed by coots and canoes in a sylvan valley painted by John Constable in 1837. Onward to the river with views of the mighty castle arresting the

GRADE: 2
ESTIMATED CALORIE BURN: 790

Description: A scenically contrasting and interest-filled walk from the tiny hamlet of South Stoke to one of the grandest and most enduring castles in England, the return path passing a recreational lake and on to the banks of the River Arun.
Distance: 5 miles.
Time: 3 hours.
Gradient: 10% of the route, the path leading from the river at point 2 and the lane at the end of point 7 climbing steeply. Three stiles.
Underfoot: The paths at points 1 and 8 can be boggy after inclement weather and the footpath is indistinct at point 3 – follow instructions.
Starting point: South Stoke on the dead-end lane verge near St Leonard's church. GR 024100.
How to get there: Arundel is immediately north of Littlehampton off the A27. Take the 'Town Centre' access off the roundabout near the railway station, cross the river and go first right on the lane below the castle. Continue uphill to the South Stoke/Offham signpost and go left and right, continuing to South Stoke.
OS map: Explorer 121 Arundel & Pulborough.
Refreshments: Teas and snacks at the Swanbourne Lodge Tea Rooms at point 4 and good bar meals at the Black Rabbit pub (see point 7).

eye, we next pass a nature reserve and reedbeds, where in summer you will hear the distinctive metallic twitters and squeaks of reed bunting. Taking leave of the river at the tempting Black Rabbit pub, we head back to South Stoke on a quiet lane and a field path.

Please note that Arundel Park – points 2 to 4 of the walk – is closed to the public on 24th March each year.

1 Walk back along the lane to the bend and turn right, passing the entrance to **South Stoke Farm**. Continue for 30 yards and turn right, following the public bridleway sign. Pass **Chapel Barn**; five-arched and brick-built, it was erected in 1860. Continue for 150 yards and go left, following a public bridleway sign, on a field edge track. In the corner, keep forward and drop down to a gate. Go through right and swing left uphill along the field edge. In the corner, keep forward, following the public bridleway sign into a wood, dropping down on a winding path, following the looping line of a boundary wall to your left. Continue to the **Arundel Park** signpost.

2 Go left through the metal kissing gate and follow the yellow arrow marker on a post, walking parallel with the boundary wall. Swing right, following a yellow arrow marker and a fence line, climbing to a footpath sign. Swing right to the next sign and go left, following the sign, on a wheel-rutted track to a gate.

3 Go through, following the yellow arrow marker into a large field and head to the right of a wood. A panorama unfolds, the elegant **Horne Tower** and the distant sea attracting the gaze. Swing broad right away from the wood and drop down into the valley bottom. Go through a gate and keep dropping down, continuing to a signpost.

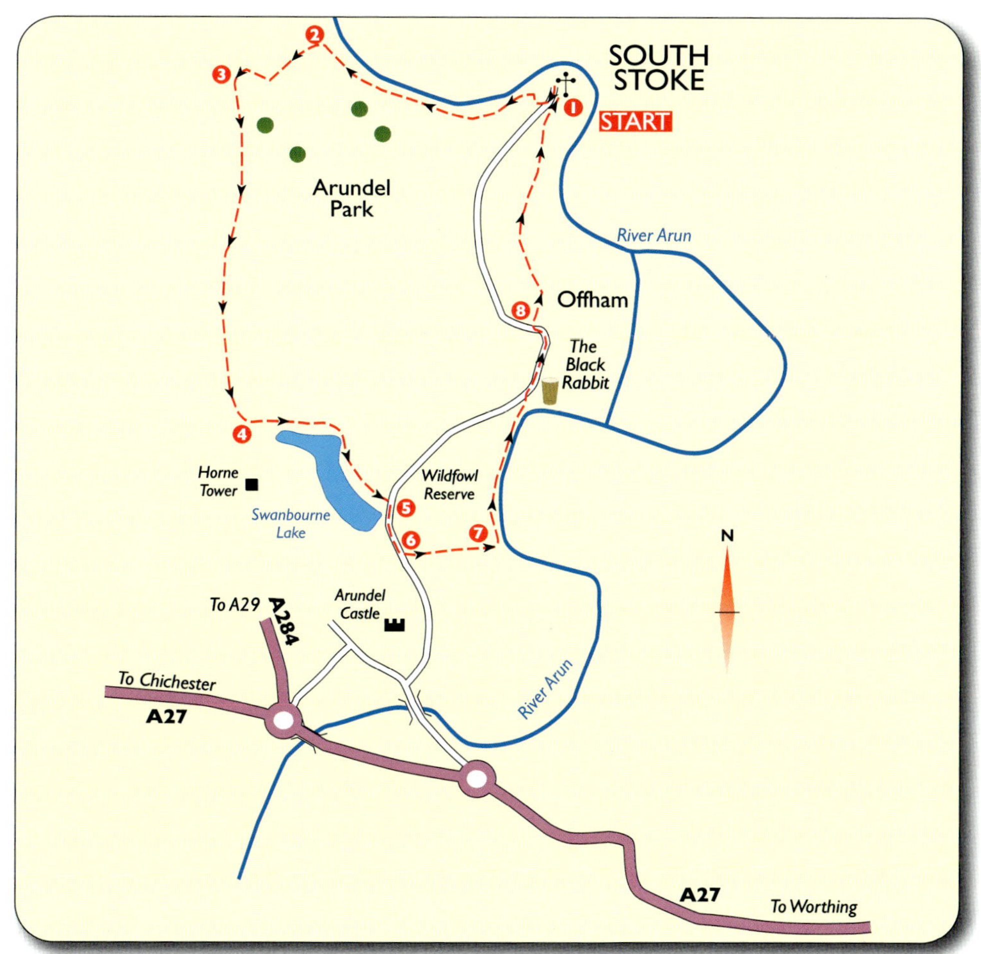

■ *Arundel castle seen towering above the treetops* ■

4 Go left along a side valley, following a yellow arrow marker and weaving left. Cross a stile by a lake and follow a yellow arrow marker forward, swinging right by the lake bank. Continue to the **Swanbourne Lodge Tea Rooms**.

5 Turn right along the lane and walk on towards the bridge.

6 Turn left immediately before the bridge, following a public footpath sign, and walk down to the **Arun riverbank** and the tri-directional sign. There are magnificent views of **Arundel Castle** from here.

7 Turn left along the riverbank, passing the reedbeds and the nature reserve. Walk on upstream to the **Black Rabbit pub**. Go left of the pub and immediately right on the lane, climbing up a deep ferny bank to the **South Stoke/Offham** sign and go left for 120 yards.

8 Go right off the lane, following a sign through a gate, and drop down, passing a cottage called **Foxes Oven**. Cross a second stile and keep forward at the next sign, crossing a third stile by a gate. Swing left uphill and continue to the lane, going right back to the start.

16 West Hoathly
Lodestones

FOOTPATHS FOR FITNESS

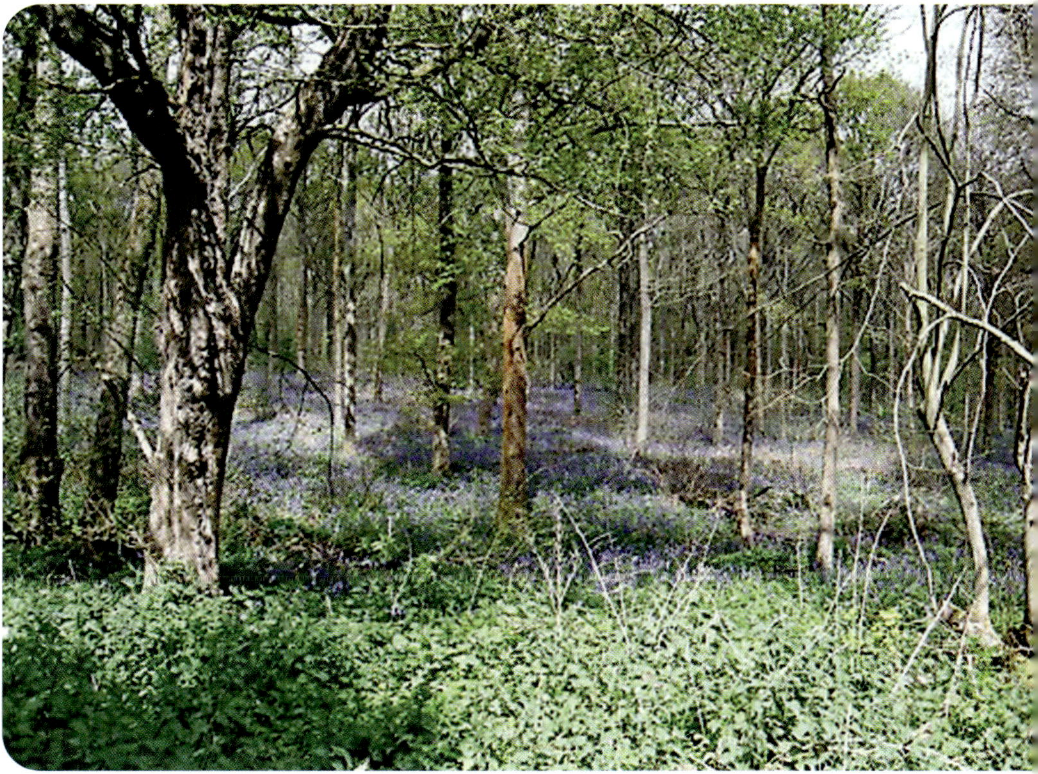

■ *Springtime in the woods* ■

In the mists of time, centuries before the Industrial Revolution, the Sussex Weald put a roar in the lion that would become England, the county's smelt mills providing hot iron by the ton. Long before the industry gave rise to West Hoathly village, there was an extensive hill fort at nearby Philpots that guarded local mines. Coveted by the Romans, these and others in the Weald were the main source of metal for military and civilian use during the occupation. The industry flourished and, in 1283, the Sheriff of Sussex was ordered by royal decree to furnish the army with 30,000 horseshoes and 60,000 nails, the profitable industry making local ironmasters, such as the Infields of Gravetye, rich. Much of the fabric of modern West Hoathly is

GRADE: 2
ESTIMATED CALORIE BURN: 935

Description: A quiet country lanes and woodland tracks hike on part of the High Weald Landscape Trail, passing ancient sites associated with the iron industry.
Distance: 5½ miles.
Time: 3 hours.
Gradient: 40% of the route, at points 2 to 8 and particularly at point 5.
Underfoot: Some of the paths, particularly those near water in shaded woodland areas, can be muddy after heavy rain.
Starting point: Park on North Lane opposite the church. GR 363326.
How to get there: West Hoathly is around 4½ miles south-west of East Grinstead and around the same distance south-east from junction 10A of the M23 on a minor road east of the B2028 between Ardingly and Turners Hill.
OS map: Explorer 135 Ashdown Forest.
Refreshments: The Cat Inn opposite the church (not open on Mondays) serves highly recommended bar meals. Also see the notes about the hospitality offered by St Margaret's church in point 8.

derived from the trade, many of its cottages and manor houses and its ancient church resounding to the ring of iron.

This fascinating walk, largely through woodlands awash with bluebells, cuckoo flowers and wild garlic during the spring season, follows the Iron Age compass all the way, visiting the 15th-century, timber-framed Priest House, the long discarded iron founders' pits and dams, and the 11th-century church of St Margaret.

The Priest House is in the ownership of Sussex Past and has been open as a museum since 1908. It displays a varied collection of 17th- and 18th-century ironwork, furniture, textiles and domestic bygones. In the doorway is a rough iron slab from a local furnace. The slab is supposed to stop witches entering the house, which is open from March until early November (telephone: 01342 810479).

1 Follow the lane down past the **Priest House**. Swing right on the bend, pass the bowling green and continue to the next bend. Keep straight on, following the public bridleway sign down a single-track road, passing **Philpots Lodge**. Pass the working quarry and the school.

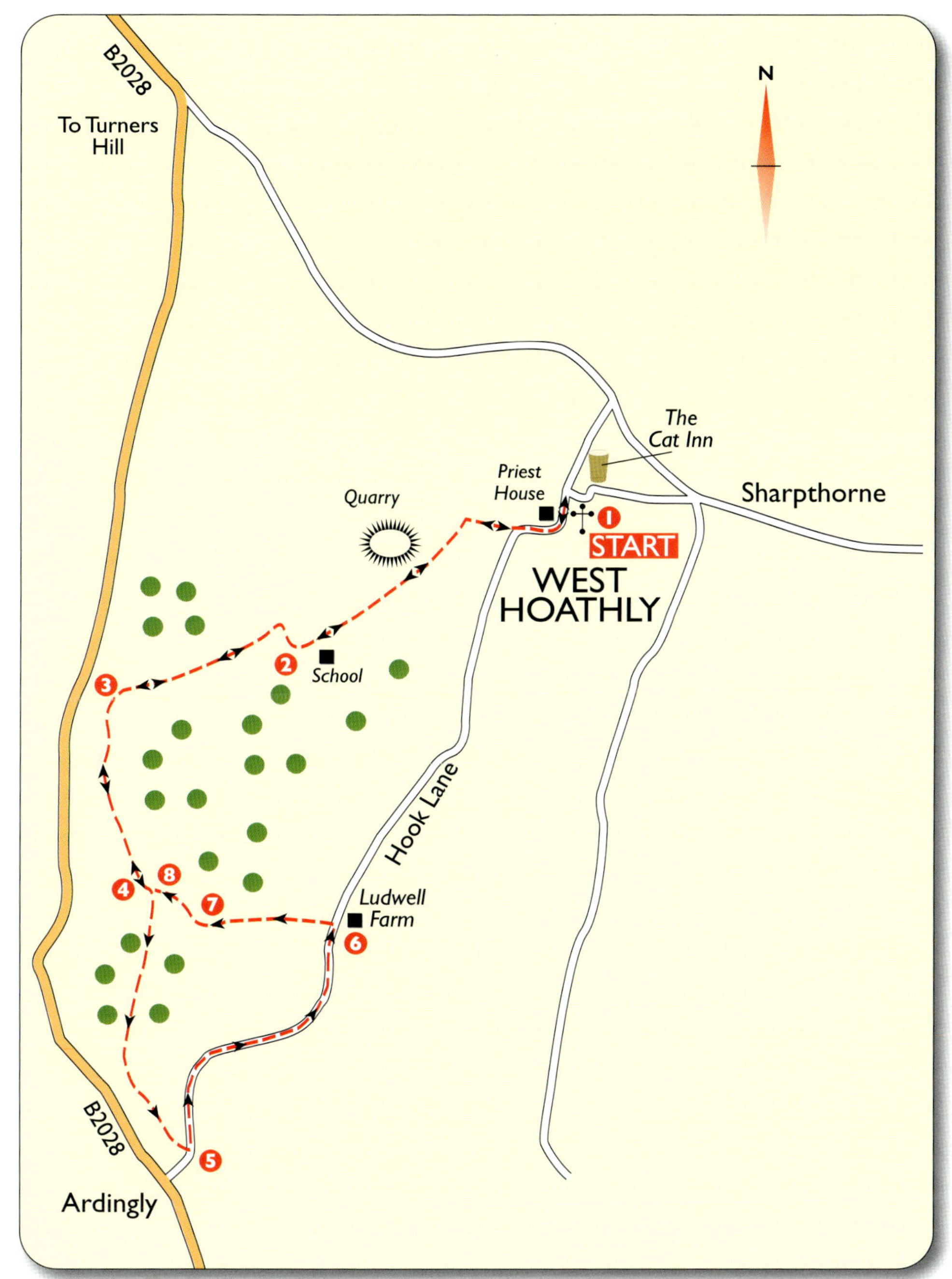

N
B2028
To Turners Hill
The Cat Inn
Priest House
Sharpthorne
Quarry
START
1
WEST HOATHLY
2
School
3
Hook Lane
8
4
7
Ludwell Farm
6
B2028
5
Ardingly

■ *The Priest House, now a museum* ■

2 Swing right at the public bridleway sign between the buildings and drop down left on a path into woodland. The dams and conduits in the bottom are remnants of the old smelting industry. Follow the path and cross a track and follow the public bridleway sign uphill, swinging left.

3 On reaching the shale track in the clearing, fork right, following the bridleway/public footpath sign, and follow the public bridleway sign left fenceside. Swing right uphill and enter the wood, continuing to the tri-directional sign.

4 Go left downhill, following the public bridleway sign to **Hook Lane**.

5 Go left on the quiet lane and drop steeply down, crossing the stream and rising steeply up, passing **Horncombe**. Walk on for ½ mile, continuing for 20 yards past the **Ludwell Farm** sign.

6 Go left off the lane, following the public footpath sign through a gate, and follow the hedge down. In the field corner go through the gate and forward over a field, keeping left of the pond in the bottom.

7 Follow the footpath sign through a fence opening into a wood and drop down right to a footbridge. Cross and climb up right to signposts and the outward route.

8 Turn right on the outward route back into the village and visit the church.

Is St Margaret's the only church in Christendom to offer strangers like me free refreshments? I've never encountered such hospitality before! There's a sign on an old chest to the left of the porch that invites visitors to help themselves to tea and coffee. This wonderful church is full of reminders of the village's iron industry, artefacts including the nails that pick out the date 'March 31 1626' on the front door, old iron clockworks which formerly hung in the tower and were probably gifted by the local wealthy ironmasters, and iron grave slabs which commemorate the Infields – ironmasters of Gravetye to the north of the village.

Take my arm and I will lead you there,
Your lowered lids shut tight.
Hush, be still, tread light and hark,
The breaking cuckoo calls proclaim a woodland sprite.
Like unseen heralds those foul and pungent ramsons
Announce the flowered queen,
But bidden blind, abide until
I part the purdahed green.
Now look and gasp in eye-stabbed awe,
All joy and wonder reeling,
Our Rule-Britannia bloom amassed in swaying ranks,
Her blue-burst bells all pealing.

Len Markham: *Old England's Glory* – conceived in a
wood near West Hoathly opposite the Royal Botanic
Gardens and the Millennium Seedbank

17 South Harting
Paradise Down

■ *Whitcombe Bottom at point 6 of the route* ■

In **an age of rapid change** and uncertainty, the National Trust bestrides the British countryside like a god, its hand of immortality casting permanent spells on some of the most precious landscapes in Britain. And landscapes come no more precious than the 550-acre Harting Down, as uplifting and joyously beautiful a place as I have enjoyed in over 1,000 miles on foot.

From a height of nearly 800 ft, there is nothing to offend the eye in a 50-mile, orbit-spinning span of West Sussex and her sister counties; a procession of unfolding panoramas gloriously culminating in views of the sea and the Isle of Wight. Grieving parents gave Harting Down to the National Trust in 1987 in memory of a beloved son. Myriads of sculpted monuments could be no more heart-rending or valuable than this. Your hike will be attended by birdsong for most of its length and, like me, you may encounter buzzards in Whitcombe Bottom. The area is also home to nightingales, rare grasses and orchids, the Duke of Burgundy butterfly, fallow deer and adders.

GRADE: 3
ESTIMATED CALORIE BURN: 1,065

Description: A strenuous up-the-downs roller-coaster ride, the varied topography including woodland, a ruined belvedere tower, open hills with panoramic views of villages, farmland and the sea, and a sleepy pastoral hollow that will make you believe you have wandered into Elysium.

Distance: 6 miles.

Time: 4 hours.

Gradient: The route involves some serious climbing at points 1, 2, 3, 4 and 7. One stile.

Underfoot: All the paths are generally even and well maintained.

Starting point: South Harting village. Roadside parking opposite the White Hart Inn. GR 785195.

How to get there: South Harting is on the B2146 south-east of Petersfield. Approaching from Chichester (around 10 miles to the south-east), take the A286 north and go through Mid Lavant, forking left on the B2141 to South Harting.

OS map: Explorer 120 Chichester.

Refreshments: Near the parking area, the White Hart Inn and the Ship are both recommended for bar meals.

1 Walk towards the **church of St Mary and St Gabriel** on the pavement and keep forward on the road (caution: no footway for 130 yards). At the bend keep forward, following a public footpath sign and a blue arrow marker (hidden by a tree to the right), and go through a gate into a municipal park. Follow a winding path through woodland, climbing up to the footpath signs. Keep ascending forward and continue in the same direction at the next yellow arrow-marked post. Go through the gap by the gate near the top and cross the B2146 left, following the **South Downs Way** sign. Follow the winding wooded path up to the B2141. (If you wish to view the ruined gazebo to the right on **Tower Hill**, weave right through the wood to the pasture edge.)

2 Cross the road left and enter the signed '**Harting Down Local Nature Reserve**'. Keep going forward and through a gate, following the **South Downs Way** sign. Follow the blue arrow marker on a post by the summit copse to your left and go forward at the next post, following the blue arrow marker. Keep on the broad track dropping down left to the bottom and climb steeply up right. Swing right to the triangulation pillar on **Beacon Hill**; this was the site of a shutter telegraph station between 1796 and 1816, the telegraph chain linking the Admiralty in London with ships in Plymouth and Portsmouth. Go left, descending to the public bridleway sign, and continue dropping down to the '**Harting Down Local Nature Reserve**' sign.

3 Turn sharp right on an ascending track and at the top, keep forward at the **South Downs Way** sign, walking on to a tri-directional sign.

4 Turn right on a track, following the **South Downs Way** sign and a blue arrow marker. Go through a gate and walk on to a direction post.

5 Go left off the main track, following a blue arrow marker downhill, heading in the direction of the sea. Drop down to the post in the bottom and turn right by the pond.

6 Go left through a gate into the heavenly **Whitcombe Bottom** on a track and climb up steadily right. Near the crest, ignore the track to the left and keep forward to the still visible earthworks known as **Cross Dykes**. It is thought that the gated dyke was a sort of 'checkpoint' for people and animals passing along the ridge.

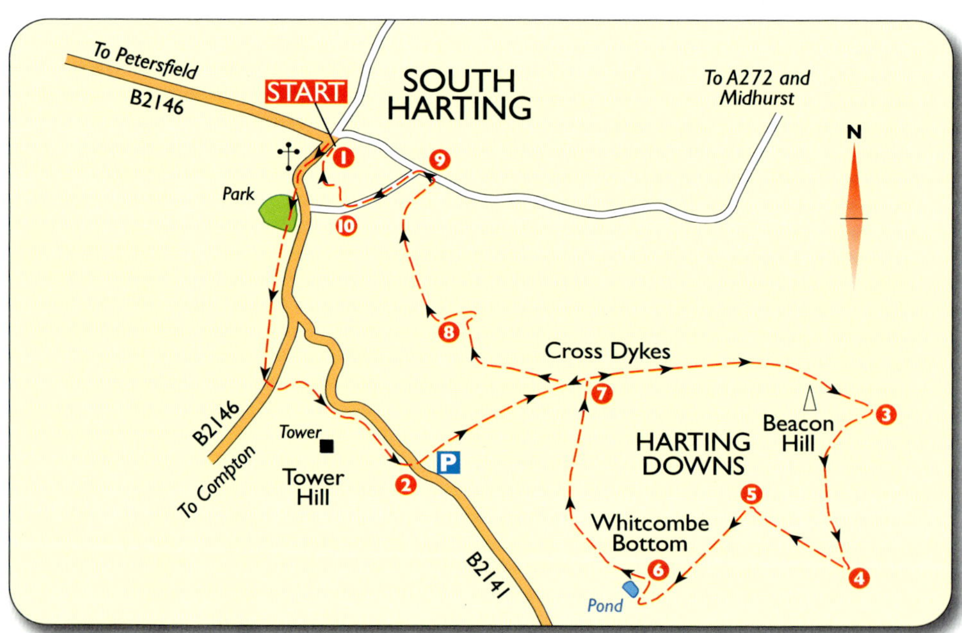

■ *The ruin atop Tower Hill* ■

7 Go left on the outward route for 200 yards and fork right off the crest, dropping downhill to a tri-directional sign. Ignore the right turn (path overgrown) and keep forward to the next sign, turning right downhill. Cross a stile and drop down the steps to **Hill Lane**.

8 Turn right for 10 yards and go left on a track, swinging right downhill. Keep forward on **New Lane** and walk on to the junction.

9 Go left for 100 yards and go left again on **Tipper Lane** and walk on to the school.

10 Turn right on a path by the new cottages with the school to your left (at the no cycling sign) and go next left by the village hall, following the weaving path back to the starting point.

After reaching South Harting and taking his leave of his three friends in *The Four Men*, Hilaire Belloc '… went in gloom by the nearest spur onto the grass and into the loneliness of the high Downs that are my brothers and my repose …'.

18 Bosham and Fishbourne

Patrician Paths

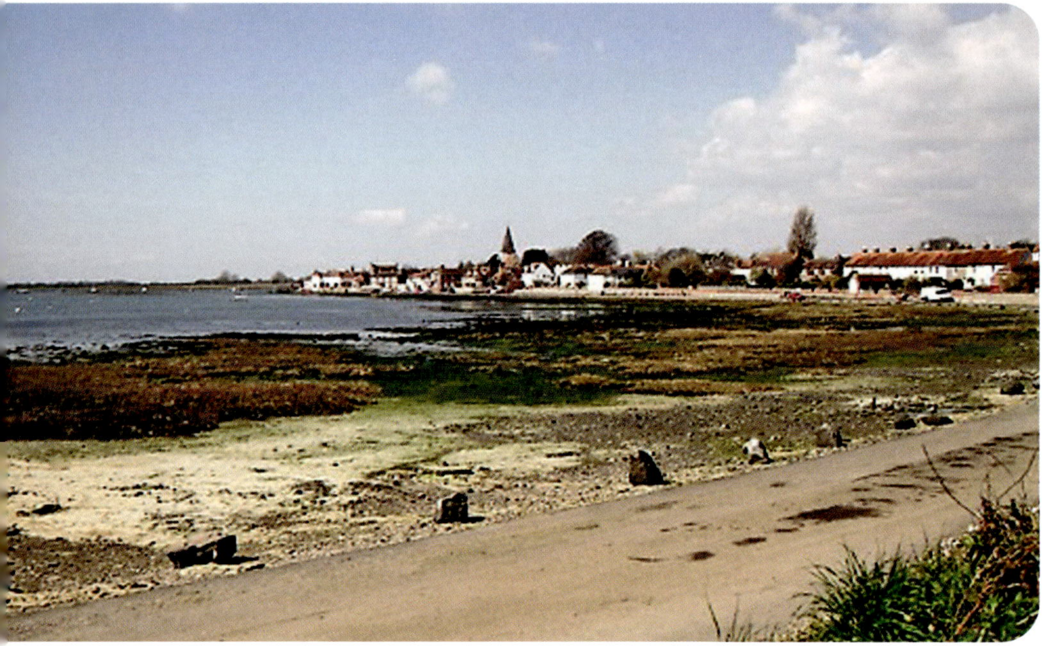

■ *The path back to Bosham* ■

Trim your boots with ermine for this regal ramble across low-lying pastures lapped by the Bosham and Chichester channels, our Olympian way leading from a harbour long associated with King Harold and the Emperor Vespasian to a remarkably preserved and magnificent Roman palace which was one of the most opulent in the province of Britannia.

Our walk first explores the delightful village of Bosham, visiting its quayside, old mill and Saxon church, the route heading east along the edge of a creek and over farmland to a raised causeway and on through reed-fringed marshes where you may see rare birds such as white egrets. Passing a millpond, the path takes us to the flower-filled Fishbourne Meadows and on to Fishbourne and the Roman palace, the return track using field paths back to Bosham.

Fishbourne Roman Palace is open at weekends throughout the year and daily from the end of January until mid December (telephone: 01243 785859).

GRADE: 3
ESTIMATED CALORIE BURN: 900

Description: A fairly long – but gradient free – villages, creeks and farmland ramble packed with historical connections, much of the route encompassing unspoilt and protected wildlife habitats.
Distance: 6 miles.
Time: 3 hours.
Gradient: The route is flat all the way.
Underfoot: All the paths are clearly defined but the land is low-lying and some small stretches are prone to flooding (although there are an adequate number of crossings and bridges) in wet weather and at high tide. The foreshore Waterfront Road is covered at high water but a raised walkway keeps the boots dry.
Starting point: Park in the pay and display car park signposted left of Bosham Lane as you approach Waterfront Road. GR 806040.
How to get there: Bosham is about 3 miles west of Chichester. Leave the A259 at Broad Bridge roundabout and go south on the minor road for 1 mile, following the signs.
OS map: Explorer 120 Chichester.
Refreshments: The Anchor Bleu inn on High Street in Bosham serves good bar food and daily specials. It has an inviting patio garden. The Palace Café in the grounds of the Roman palace serves inexpensive snacks.

1 From the car park, follow the sign to the harbour and the village and turn left on **Bosham Lane**. Turn right at the water's edge (it is prone to flooding at high tide) on **Waterfront Road** and proceed past the **Anchor Bleu inn** and the watermill to the quay. Swing right over **Quay Meadow** and pass **Holy Trinity church**. This is depicted in the Bayeux Tapestry, one panel (replica inside) showing King Harold kneeling to pray in the church before his unsuccessful journey to Normandy to intercede with William the Conqueror in 1064.

Continue on to **Bosham Lane** and turn right to the water's edge.

2 Turn left using the raised walkway above the road and walk on, swinging right to the end of the creek.

3 Go left by the bench, crossing the lane, and follow the public footpath sign between gardens. Cross **Taylor's Lane** and keep forward, following the signs across fields to **Old Park Lane**. Keep forward to the next junction of tracks.

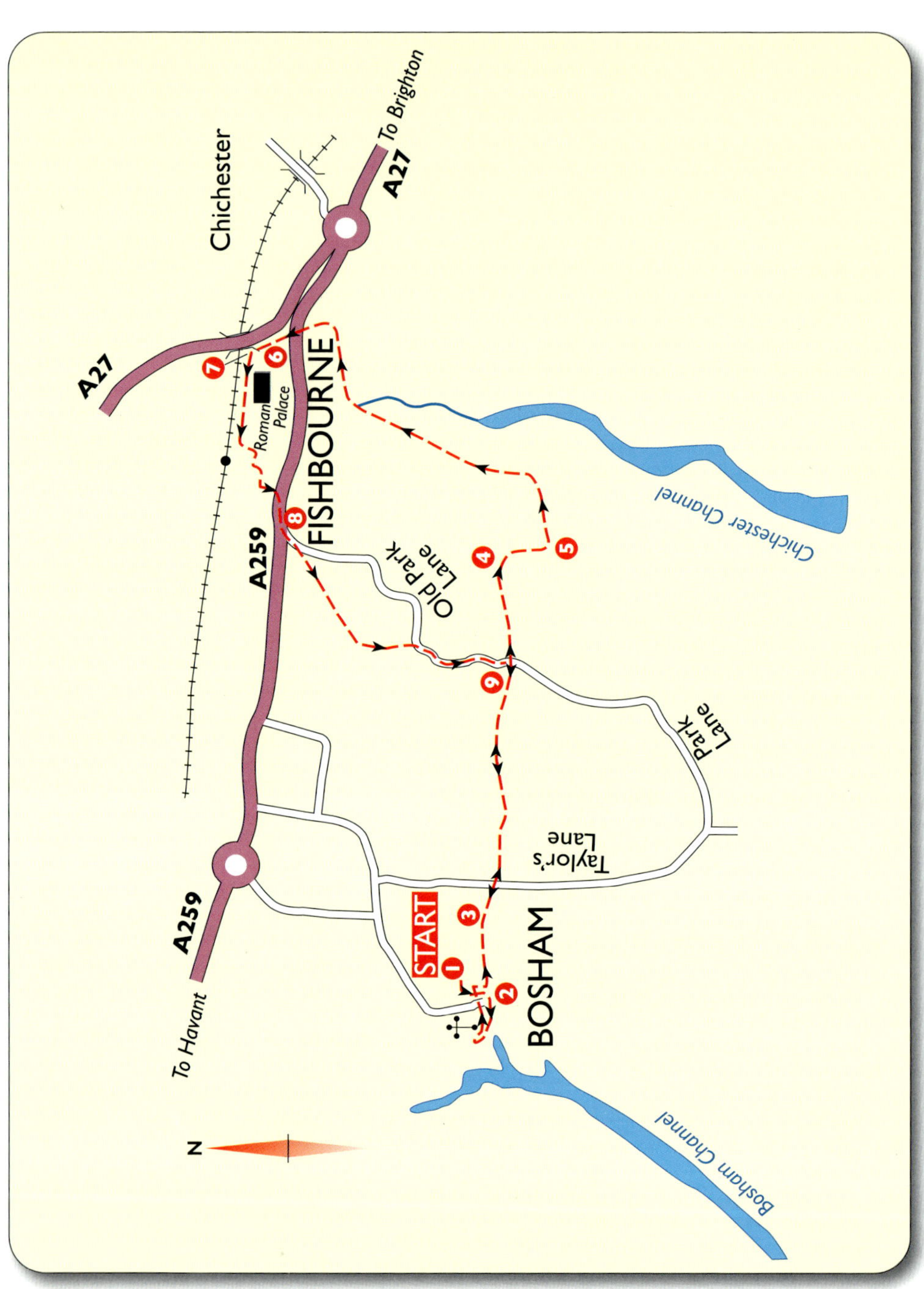
To Brighton
A27
Chichester
A27
FISHBOURNE
Roman Palace
7
6
8
A259
Old Park Lane
Chichester Channel
4
5
9
Park Lane
Taylor's Lane
To Havant
A259
START
1
3
2
BOSHAM
Bosham Channel
N

4 Turn right along a field edge, following a public footpath sign, to the drainage ditch.

5 Go left, following the sign along the ditch, heading for the channel, and cross the planked bridges over the marshy land. Swing left by the pond and go left up the steps onto the raised causeway. Follow the signs over the three bridges, swinging right by the old millpond. Keep straight forward through the kissing gate, following the millstream. Enter **Fishbourne Meadows** and swing right over the boardwalk and left over the bridge. Keep right over the concreted crossing and left, following the public footpath sign opposite the church, going through a kissing gate. Cross a footbridge and continue to the A259.

■ *Fishbourne's mill pond* ■

6 Cross and keep forward, going through a gate on a metalled track and walk on, passing the **Roman palace grounds** to your left.

7 Go left and pass the palace entrance and keep forward on **Roman Way**, passing the **Fishbourne Primary School**, swinging left to the lane. Go left for 150 yards and go right opposite **West View**, following the **Bosham Cycle Route** sign down a cul-de-sac towards playing fields. Go left on a track at the back of the houses and swing right at the bottom of the playing field, then swing left to the A259. Turn right using the footway opposite **Bosham clinic** and walk on.

8 Just past the telephone box, fork left down **Old Park Lane** and at the bend keep straight ahead, following the public footpath sign. Go left at the next signpost towards the lane, passing **Withy Cottage**, and keep forward on the lane to the footpath signs.

9 Go right on the outward route back to Bosham.

19 East Dean
The Hind Quarters

■ *East Dean – as pretty as a picture* ■

Such are the beguiling delights of one of the prettiest and most relaxing villages in the county (and the local pub serves real ale and has a shellfish bar for goodness sake!) that the inclusion of this walk should come with a chide to 'shake a leg!' So onward, our route taking us along a quiet lane, through a beautiful open vale that in ancient times was used for extensive agriculture and on through the solitude of extensively forested hillsides to join the South Downs Way at the top of Graffham Down.

For a while, we follow the densely wooded crest path with its profusion of wild flowers, including foxglove, hemp agrimony and great mullein, passing several open access wildlife reserves cared for by the Graffham Down Trust. We then plunge back into the forest on the return to the village by way of a graveyard for old farm vehicles and the entrance to a cabinet-maker's workshop that advertises itself by way of a remarkable totem pole.

The overwhelming ambience of this walk is one of complete tranquillity

GRADE: 3
ESTIMATED CALORIE BURN: 1060

Description: A forest circular to the top of Graffham Down.
Distance: 6½ miles.
Time: 3 hours.
Gradient: 25% of the route, mainly at points 4, 6 and 7. No stiles.
Underfoot: Good shale tracks for most of the way through the forested areas, two field-edge footpaths and a quiet lane.
Starting point: Park on-street outside the chapel by the village pond and green. GR 903129.
How to get there: East Dean is around 10 miles north-east of Chichester and can be accessed either from the A285 or A286. The easiest route is from the A285 at Singleton, going east through Charlton.
OS map: Explorer 121 Arundel & Pulborough.
Refreshments: The inviting Star and Garter in East Dean serves excellent bar and restaurant meals, specialising in fresh seafood. It has its own shellfish bar and an attractive beer garden.

and peace away from all distractions, the sight of my first deer – and then along came two more – in over a thousand miles of walking in Sussex underlining the completely unspoilt nature of the countryside around East Dean.

1 Walk away from the pond on the lane, passing the **Star and Garter**, and continue uphill past the village hall and the entrance to **All Saints' church**. This historic building is well worth a visit. Set into the exterior wall of the south transept is an interesting Sussex marble grave slab remembering master sword-maker William Peachey (died 1688) of East Dean who supplied weapons to Oliver Cromwell's officers during the English Civil War. Walk on to the signposts and the junction with **Newhouse Lane**.

2 Go left along the lane for 100 yards and turn right, following the public bridleway sign. Turn left at the **Hebron Cottage** sign along a track between the houses and a field and merge with **Newhouse Lane**, swinging right and keeping forward for 250 yards.

3 Turn right, following a public footpath sign fieldside, and walk up to the edge of woodland and a track.

4 Turn left along the track and continue, climbing up to the **Charlton Forest/Riphook/New Road** sign.

5 Go left (no sign) on a woodland/field edge path downhill and turn right at the tri-directional sign, following the blue arrow marker. Walk on to a point immediately above **Postles Barn** to the left. Drop down left through the fringe of the wood to the barn.

6 Turn right on a farm track and go through a gate, following a blue arrow marker, forking right on the higher track, walking parallel with the farm

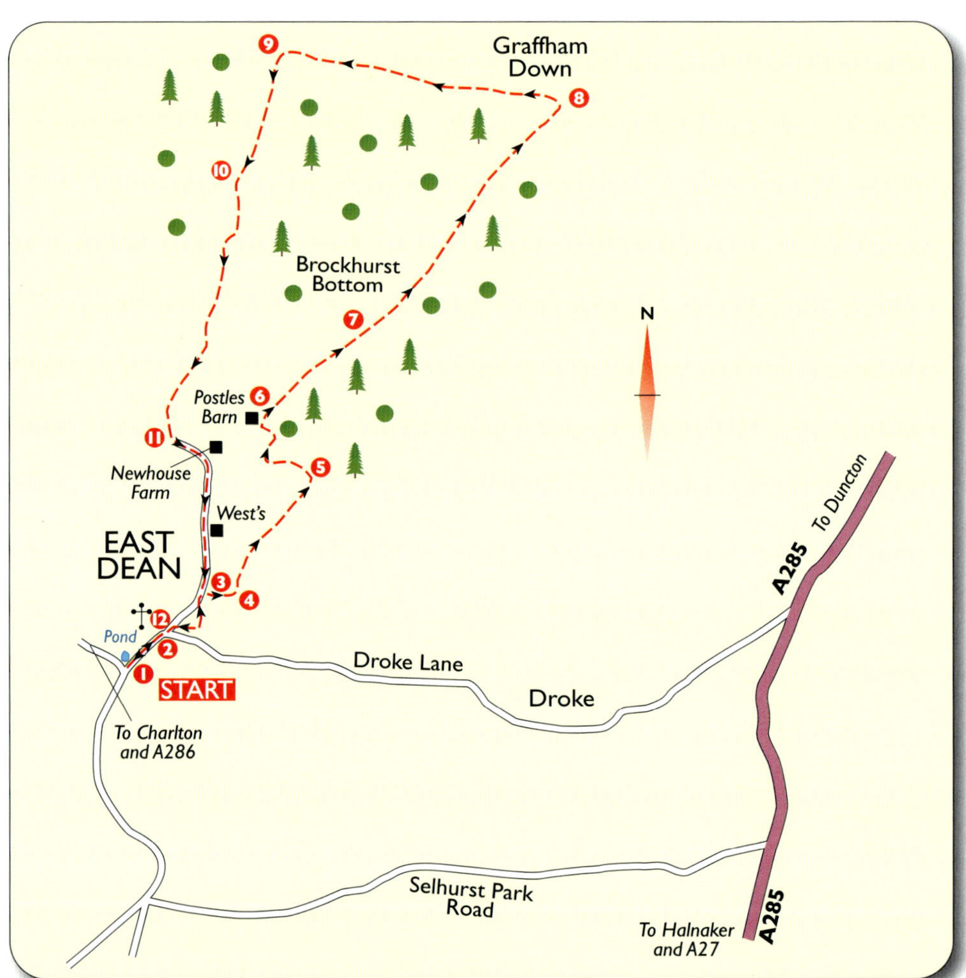

track. Merge with the farm track and keep forward at the first of the big beech trees, continuing through a gate to the direction post.

7 Follow the purple arrow marker, taking the path left into **Brockhurst Bottom**, and continue slightly right uphill to the right of the conifers. Go through a gate, following the purple arrow marker, and walk on uphill through the forest, keeping forward at the cross tracks and ascending to the **South Downs Way** signs at the top of **Graffham Down**.

■ *Out of steam at East Dean* ■

8 Go left, following the **South Downs Way** sign along a crest track. At the next set of signs, keep forward, passing the gated entrance to **Bowley's Field**. Keep going forward at the next three sets of signs.

9 At the fourth set of signs, go left off the crest track back into the forest, following the blue arrow marker on a descending track, walking on over a cross track. Where the track forks by the turning area, keep forward, ignoring the right track, and continue for 150 yards.

10 Go left, following the tri-directional bridleway sign, and drop down on a winding track, going forward at the next blue arrow marker and weaving right near the edge of the forest and left through a gate to the farm buildings.

11 Go right on the lane, passing the rusting farm machinery and building plant, and weave left, passing **Newhouse Farm** on **Newhouse Lane**. Pass the totem pole outside the premises of **West's** furniture manufacturers and follow the outward route back to the junction.

12 Turn right along the lane back to the starting point.

20 Chanctonbury and Cissbury

FOOTPATHS FOR FITNESS

Lord of the Rings

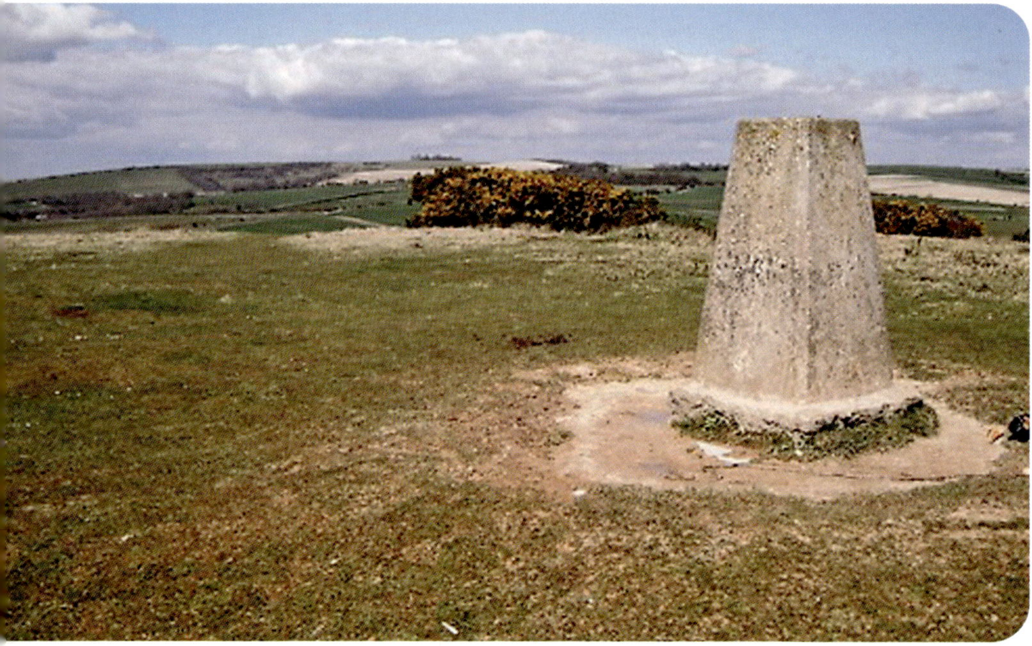

■ *The view from Cissbury Ring* ■

Study this walk on the map and be transported to a realm as mystical as any creation of Tolkien's, the notations in antique fonts – *ring*, *fort*, *tumuli*, *dyke* and *flint mines* – setting the ancestral time-machine spinning wildly into reverse, unleashing a pantheon of lords and demons. I defy you to let your eye linger on the Ordnance Survey sheet and not resolve to visit the compelling hilltop redoubts of Chanctonbury and Cissbury rings in one glorious if somewhat strenuous day, thousand year old ghosts leading you all the way along ancient trackways on a timeless pilgrimage. And all this before you've even seen the view from the start!

Chanctonbury Ring girdles an Iron Age hill fort, once the later site of a Romano-Celtic temple. At a height of 800 ft, the eminence commands fabulous views of almost the entire county with glimpses of the Seven Sisters and distant Hampshire and Kent. For the best part of two centuries, this much-loved Sussex peak was clothed with a stand of beech trees planted

GRADE: 3
ESTIMATED CALORIE BURN: 1,360

Description: Linked by an arrow-straight causeway, a panorama-spinning, lung-testing hike between two of the most iconic hilltops in Sussex, our route orbiting the twin sites.
Distance: 8½ miles.
Time: 4½ hours.
Gradient: 20% of the route; acclivity pronounced in point 4 and point 5, the back track climbing steadily in point 8.
Underfoot: Most of the route is on firm stone and turf tracks but the woodland paths, particularly on the approach to Chanctonbury Ring, can be very muddy after rain.
Starting point: The free picnic site car park at the end of Chanctonbury Ring Road. GR 146125.
How to get there: The car park is ¾ mile down Chanctonbury Ring Road and is signposted south off the A283 between Washington and Bramber.
OS map: Explorer 121 Arundel & Pulborough.
Refreshments: There are no catering establishments close by but both Chanctonbury and Cissbury are favoured spots for picnics.

and steadfastly watered and tended in 1760 by Charles Goring of Wiston, the great gale of October 1987 scything through the plantation with devastating force. Replanting is helping to ensure that Goring, at least, sleeps soundly.

Within a lightning strike of Chanctonbury and clearly seen to the south, is Cissbury, the largest and most impressive prehistoric camp on the South Downs. Some 60,000 tons of chalk were excavated in the Neolithic epoch in creating a spectacular defensive earthwork of ditches and ramparts, with a later excavation of flints on an almost industrial scale for use in weaponry and for domestic purposes employing hundreds of hewers. Some flints were even exported abroad. In later centuries, the site became an Iron Age fort, the Romans adapting it for agriculture before it was refortified to answer the threat from Saxon raiders.

1 Go left on the track for 200 yards.

2 Turn right for about ¾ mile, following a public bridleway sign, on a woodland-edge track and go through a gate, following a blue arrow marker.

Pass an old barn and swing left uphill and right and go through a second gate, following a blue arrow marker. Continue through a third gate, swinging left uphill for 100 yards to the marker post.

3 Go left, following the blue arrow marker uphill into the wood, climbing on a track and swinging left. Go through a gate and keep ascending, swinging right to the top, going through a final gate and steering left towards **Chanctonbury Ring**. Pass the newly established replacement plantation and swing right on a broad track – the **South Downs Way** – continuing to the signposts.

4 Swing right south-wards, heading for the sea (signpost missing) on a track and continue for just short of 2 miles to the **Cissbury Ring parking area**.

5 Enter the National Trust's **Cissbury Ring** through a gate and, keeping right of the litter bin, sweep left uphill on a woodland track, following a blue arrow marker. Go through a gate.

6 Turn right and enter the ring through a kissing gate, swinging left through a breach and right to a triangulation pillar. There is a good view back towards **Chanctonbury Ring** from here. Go left on a turfy track, heading towards the sea, to a second breach in the ring.

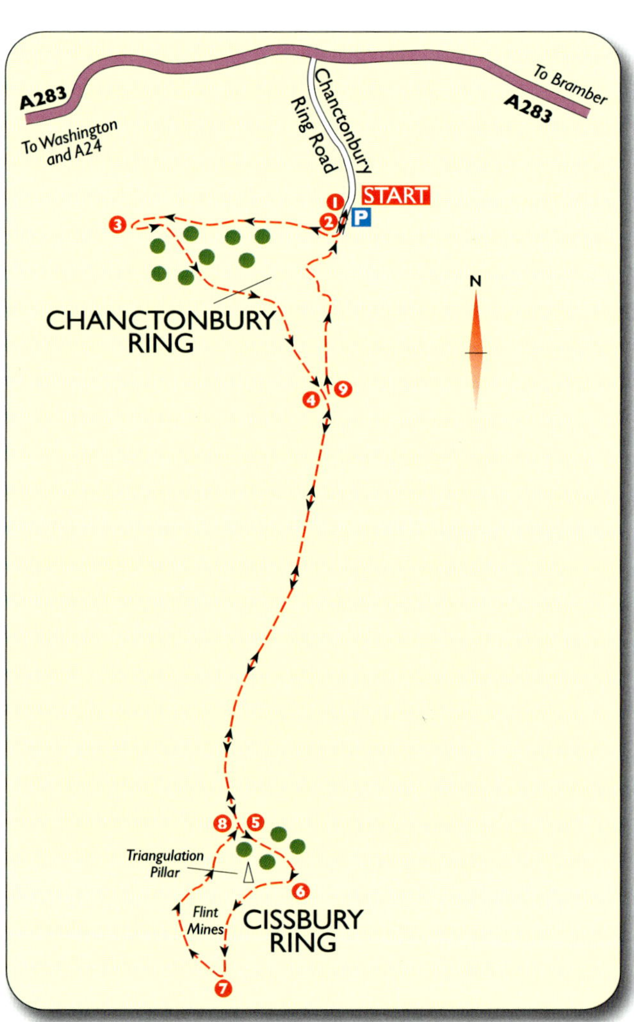

■ *On Chanctonbury Ring* ■

7 Steer right up the steps to the top of the embankment and walk clockwise around the ring, dropping down the next flight of steps left off the embankment, returning to point 5 to complete the circle.

8 Go north on the outward track, returning to the start of point 4.

9 Keep forward, following the public bridleway sign, on a descending woodland track. Swing left and swing right at the blue arrow marker and continue on the track back to the car park.

Aloft her heaven song defies the probing eye,
Unseen in the panoramic sweep, her tiny heartbeat swelling.
Alone in bleated green I stop to peer and tingle,
Straining to spot a gossamer lightship, fixed and fluttering in the blue.
I bathe in song under the feathered belfry,
The tumbling chimes of infant bells,
Falling like ear-sweet snowflakes,
As bright as lambs in April,
As skittish as a gale-tossed kite,
To melt on my lips in a whistle,
As I fling up my cap in delight!

Len Markham: *The Skylark* – excited by an audience with a
songstress at lambing time on Cissbury Ring.

Calorie Chart

The following chart shows the approximate calories spent per hour by a person weighing 8 stone (112 lbs), 11 stone (154 lbs) and 15 stone (210 lbs)

	8 stone	11 stone	15 stone
Walking, 2 mph	160	240	312
Walking, 3 mph	210	320	416
Walking, 4½ mph	295	440	572

Note that these figures are based on moderate, not vigorous, activity.

Special Offer

A signed anthology of the author's poems entitled – *The Footprints of Old Plod – Lines from the Hills* is available direct from the author at 41 Parkway, Ratton Manor, Eastbourne BN20 9DY (Price £3.50, including postage and packing).